# HAMLYN HELP YOURSELF GUIDE

# HOW TO GET PUBLISHED

## FOR ALL BUDDING AUTHORS

### NEIL WENBORN

HAMLYN

*Acknowledgements*
Extracts from   BS 5261: Part II: 1976 are reproduced with
the permission of British Standards Institution. Complete
copies of the Standard can be obtained from BSI Sales,
Linford Wood, Milton Keynes MK14 6LE, or by telephoning
BSI order line (0908) 220022.

First published in 1990 by
The Hamlyn Publishing Group Limited,
a division of the Octopus Publishing Group,
Michelin House, 81 Fulham  Road,
London SW3 6RB

Printed and bound in Great Britain by Collins, Glasgow

# Contents

## From Proposal to Contract    55

## Researching your Book    73

## Writing your Book    85

## What Happens to your Manuscript?    96

## In Print  114

## Appendices

# Introduction

It has been said that we all have a book in us somewhere. Certainly many people dream of seeing themselves in print, of the thrill of finding their work on the shelves of bookshops and libraries. Most of us would probably like to pass on to others our knowledge of a specialist subject or a hobby or the accumulated experience of our working lives.

Only too often, though, it is a dream which remains unfulfilled, not through lack of subject matter or the inability to write, but through a lack of understanding of the publishing process itself. We have all heard the rags to riches stories of people who wrote their first book, sent it in to a publisher, had it accepted and found themselves the authors of an overnight bestseller. Unfortunately, such experiences are extremely rare. For every overnight success, there are thousands of rejection letters and hundreds of would-be authors who give up in despair of ever getting into print.

This book is an attempt to explain how publishers work, what they look for in a potential publication and how to make sure that your idea for a book will meet those requirements. It explains how to approach publishers with your idea and what will happen should you be successful in having it accepted for publication. It covers every stage of the writing and publishing process, through to that exciting moment when you finally hold in your hand the book that bears your name.

This is not, however, a book about publishing fiction. It will not tell you how to get into print with a novel or a play, or with short stories or poetry. There is a firm division in the publishing world between fiction and non-fiction, and relatively few publishers specialise in both. The number of works of fiction published every year is only a small proportion of the total number of books published. And very often it is the work of non-fiction which outlasts the overnight fictional success and remains in print for years, giving its author a continuing source of income and the satisfaction of making his or her knowledge available to a wide and changing audience.

So – this book is about getting non-fiction published. Most of us spend the major part of our lives working at occupations which give us, often without our fully realising it, a fund of knowledge in a specialist area. Most of us also have hobbies or leisure interests in which we may become more than armchair experts. Many people who have published their work successfully have done so because they spotted a need for information in an area such as this, where they were already knowledgeable. Sometimes the information available in a particular field can only be found from a number of different sources and there may be scope for drawing it all together between one set of covers. Alternatively, there may be a particular aspect of a subject that has only been dealt with very scantily in published books or has not been written about for years. Or else there may already be books on your specialist subject but you feel you could write a better one yourself. These are all very good reasons for trying to get published. They are also the sort of reasons which will make a publisher take your ideas seriously. This book will help you to convert that interest into reality.

Finally, a word of warning. Many people feel that writing a book – even on a practical or academic subject – is a rather romantic experience. The image of the writer in a garret, scribbling line after line in a frenzy of inspiration, dies hard, even in this age of word-processors and profit margins. Writing a book is certainly a lonely business, but it is also very hard work. It is likely to take up all your leisure time for months or even years. Until you have put the last full stop to the final sentence, you will have to be prepared to spend as much, if not more, time at the library or the typewriter as with your family or friends.

Finding the right information, let alone finding the right words to communicate it or the right publisher to publish it, is a long and arduous task, and there will certainly be moments when you will ask yourself why on earth you started it. But when you finally see your name on the shelf of your local library or bookshop – when you sit opposite someone reading your book on the train or see a complimentary review in your professional journal – the answer will become clear.

# 1

# How Books get Published

Every book that gets published is the result of a partnership between one or more authors and a publisher. If you are hoping to get published, then, you need to understand something about the way publishers work and what they are looking for in the books, and therefore in the authors, they publish.

Publishing is a business. And increasingly, as large publishers take over smaller independent ones in the rash of acquisitions and mergers which the industry has seen in recent years, publishing is *big* business. The image of the tweed-jacketed publisher risking his all to bring unrecognised talents to the eyes of a philistine public was always a caricature. Nowadays it is almost unrecognisable.

That is not to say that publishers are not on the look-out for new authors to foster and develop. They are: a publisher who failed to find new authors would soon go out of business. Nor is it to say that they are not concerned about the quality of the books they produce. A publisher who neglected his/her existing authors or the quality of their publications might take longer to fail, but would be sure to go under in the end. But in the final analysis a publishing company, like any other other company, needs to make money if it is to survive.

It is against this criterion that publishers will decide which products to market. A publisher's products are his books (and increasingly his other information services). The difference between the products of a publishing company and those of most other companies is that a publisher's products cannot be produced without the intellectual help of third parties – authors – who may know nothing at all about publishing but who happen to know about the subjects the publisher sells information on. And this is where you come in.

## How publishers work

All publishers operate in more or less specialist markets. The largest publishers may specialise in a number of different subject areas and sell their books in a number of different countries, but they will all have their particular strengths and will be fighting to capitalise on those strengths in a very competitive market.

Publishers refer to the books they publish as their 'lists' or their 'lists of titles'. In order to remain competitive, they must continually build and develop these lists by publishing books in their specialist areas. They must be able physically to produce the books (with the help of specialist suppliers such as typesetters and printers – see Chapter 8) and they must be able to sell those books to the public, either directly by such techniques as direct mail marketing, or indirectly through bookshops, libraries, etc. (see Chapter 9, page 116). But above all they must be able to find people to write the books, and a large part of any publisher's efforts therefore goes into locating authors and signing agreements with them for books which they can publish in the future. This activity, which is the first stage of the whole publishing process, is known as commissioning, and is done by in-house staff known variously as commissioning editors, acquisitions editors, sponsoring editors or simply editors.

We shall be hearing more about commissioning editors later in this chapter (see pages 15 to 16). But first it is worth looking in a little more detail at the different parts which go to make up that curious commercial whole, the average publishing company.

# The departments within the publishing company

Looked at from one angle, publishers are service companies whose services take the form of tangible printed information. (More and more publishing companies are now also producing information in electronic form, but for the purposes of this book we shall concentrate on the printed word.) Looked at from another angle, they are manufacturing companies whose products happen to be collections of somewhat intangible ideas. The way in which most publishers are organised reflects this rather hybrid nature.

The average publishing company is divided into four main sections, although there are a number of variations within this basic framework. The four sections are:

- the editorial department
- the production department
- the marketing department
- the accounts department

Many publishers, and almost all the larger ones, will also have their own warehouse facilities for storing their books and despatching them to customers.

Let us look at what each of these departments does.

## The editorial department

The editorial department typically comprises two different editorial functions, which are sometimes separated to form two distinct departments. These are:

- (i) the commissioning editors
- (ii) the copy-editors

The work of the commissioning editors has already been outlined. Commissioning editors are perhaps the most important people in the publishing company from the point of view of the prospective author, and as such they are dealt with in greater detail below (see pages 15 to 16).

Copy-editors, who may also be known as desk editors, house editors, sub-editors or simply editors, only get involved at a later stage of the publishing process, when a completed manuscript has been received from an author and is ready to start the journey towards becoming a printed book. Once you have finished your manuscript and had it approved by the commissioning editor, the copy-editor will become your main point of contact with the publisher and there is more about what this involves later (see Chapter 8, pages 100 to 105).

Broadly speaking, though, the role of the copy-editor is to prepare your manuscript for the typesetters (see page 105). This means that he or she will go through what you have written with a fine tooth comb, making sure that it has a logical structure, checking that you have said everything in the clearest possible way and imposing what is known as 'house style' on it. (House style is each publishing house's set of rules about spelling, ranking of headings, layout of text on the page, etc. – see page 70.) The author will almost always be consulted about any queries raised by this process.

When the copy-editing is completed, the manuscript will be passed to:

**The production department**

The production team are the people who organise the typesetting, printing and binding of the books. Few publishers have the facilities to typeset, print and bind their books in-house and most deal with a range of regular suppliers who do this work for them. The production staff are responsible for ensuring that the materials, people and time are available to produce the books to the desired specifications and schedules. It is rare for authors to have any direct contact with this department. More detail is given about book production in Chapter 8.

## The marketing department

Once a book has been published, the publisher will put an enormous amount of time and effort into ensuring that it reaches the people it is meant to reach. The marketing team is responsible for organising campaigns to achieve this. They will normally be supported by a sales team who go out to the bookshops, colleges etc. with samples of the books.

Marketing campaigns vary according to the type of book the publisher is selling, but most fall into one or both of two basic approaches:

● direct sales

● trade sales

Direct sales are generally made by mailing information about books directly to individuals or by placing coupon advertisements or loose inserts in journals and magazines. These techniques tend to be used mainly by publishers producing books for the professional market or for other easily identifiable specialist groups. Some such publishers are now also starting to use telephone selling techniques, particularly for books such as directories.

Trade sales are those which are made to bookshops, library suppliers and other retailers. All publishers sell to these sorts of outlet, although for some types of book, such as looseleaf manuals, bookshop sales may account for a very small proportion of the total number of copies sold.

In addition to direct and trade sales, publishers often sell books to other publishers or to book clubs. Such sales usually involve the sale or licence of certain publishing rights and are also usually the responsibility of the marketing team.

There is more about the marketing of books in Chapter 9 (see pages 115 to 117). The extent to which authors have any contact with marketing staff varies according to the type of book and the type of publisher.

## The accounts department

The role of the accounts department is very similar to that of an accounts department in any company selling goods or services. It is responsible for the day-to-day financial running of the company, including customer liaison and credit control. Perhaps more important from the author's point of view is the fact that it also deals with the calculation and payment of author's royalties! The accounts department will often operate in close liaison with the warehouse.

# Commissioned books

It is often thought that books get published by authors writing complete manuscripts and sending them in to a publishing company which then recognises them as great works and rushes them into print. While this does happen, it is far from being the typical picture.

### *The role of the commissioning editor*

In technical and reference publishing the majority of the books published by any given company will probably be based on ideas thought up by the company's commissioning editors, who have then sought out the best people to write about them. A firm specialising in, say, practical guides for the business person may develop almost all its books in this way. After all, most business people will be too busy running their businesses to have time to write complete books on marketing or financial management and very few such manuscripts are therefore likely to arrive on the commissioning editor's desk in the course of the average month. Of those which do, fewer still will be publishable in their present form, if at all.

In other areas, such as academic publishing for students sitting college courses, more books will arrive unsolicited, but only a small proportion of these will be accepted for publication and those which are will often have been fought over by a number of publishers. It will still be a major part of the commissioning editor's job to go out 'into the field' and find authors, either by persuading people who are working on a book to sign an agreement with their company or by persuading people who may seldom have thought of writing a book at all to write one on a subject of the commissioning editor's choosing. In other words, most works of non-fiction get published by publishers spotting a gap in the market and finding a product to fill it.

### What commissioning editors look for

Although you may never find yourself in the fortunate position of being approached by a publisher's commissioning editor to write a book, it is worth knowing a little more about what this process involves, because it gives some vital clues as to what a publisher will be looking for from a potential author. And what a commissioning editor will ask for at this stage from a potential author whom he/she has sought out is also what he/she will be most interested in receiving as an unsolicited proposal.

The most important thing to remember is that commissioning editors will not initially ask potential authors for a complete manuscript. At first the publisher will be looking for a detailed proposal for a book, running to perhaps half a dozen sheets of A4 typescript, not a finished draft of 250 sheets. Either now or at a later stage, the publisher may also ask for a draft of one or two chapters as sample material.

The same basic principle applies if you are approaching a publisher with an unsolicited proposal. Do not spend months writing a complete book and then send it to a publisher. Always put together a package of material designed to sell your *idea* to the company you decide to approach. This will save both your and the publisher's time and will immediately strike the publisher as a professional approach.

Getting this package right is one of the most important keys to getting published, and there is much more later about what it should include (see Chapter 4). Now, though, it is worth looking in a little more detail at the part unsolicited material plays in the publishing process.

## Unsolicited material

What has been said so far may make you wonder whether you stand any chance at all of getting your idea for a book taken up by a publisher. If most publishers know precisely what they want and where to find suitable authors, can a prospective writer ever really hope to break in with a new idea?

The answer is categorically Yes.

Remember: publishing is a business and publishers are in business to make money. The business of non-fiction publishing is the business of making ideas available, at a profit, to as many people who are interested in those ideas as possible. Commissioning editors, each usually with his or her own specialist list to manage and expand, are continually on the look-out for new ideas to develop into books. And no commissioning editor worth his or her salt is going to turn down flat a proposal which may make a successful book, wherever it comes from.

There is no doubt, of course, that you will start off at a considerable advantage in getting a publisher to take you seriously as a potential author if you are a well-known expert on the subject you choose to write about, especially if you are used to broadcasting or speaking regularly at conferences and seminars as well. Your reputation will not only be some guarantee of the quality of the material you write, but will be likely to help sales as well. There will also be kudos for the company in publishing the work of such a guru (not to mention kudos – and a useful notch on the career ladder – for the editor who signs you up!).

But there is equally no reason why you should not be able to convince the potential publisher of your qualifications for writing a book if you have had a reasonable amount of experience in the field, have read widely on the subject, have something individual and important to say about it and are able to say it in a way that the publisher thinks will appeal to the market.

If there really is a market for your book, and if you can show the publisher that you are able to make a good job of writing it, there is no reason to think that you will not get it published in the end. It may take some time, and the road into print may be littered with countless rejections, but there will almost certainly be somone somewhere prepared to publish a book which is genuinely saleable.

Your job, as a potential author, is to persuade the publisher that yours is such a book. Chapters 2, 3 and 4 are designed to help you do just that.

## Literary agents

Before leaving the question of how books come to be published it is worth looking briefly at the role of literary agents.

Literary agents act as professional middlemen between authors and publishers. In return for a percentage of the money paid to the author by the publishers they will relieve the author of the burdensome business of seeking out publishers and physically sending proposals. They will also advise a prospective author on ways of making his or her material more marketable, and will help him or her negotiate terms with the publisher once a book has been accepted in principle. Few agents charge for placing a manuscript with a publisher. However, some may charge a fee for reading the manuscript, which is refundable once it has been accepted for publication.

Literary agents, like publishers' commissioning editors, are always looking for new authors and will be very helpful and supportive if they feel a work has real potential. On the whole, though, there is probably little point in employing the services of a literary agent to place your first book with a publisher. The sort of research and approach suggested in Chapters 2, 3 and 4 should enable you to identify likely publishers yourself and help you to put together the sort of proposal that will catch their attention and make them take you seriously. (Later, when you have published successfully and have publishers queueing up for your work, things may be different. Unfortunately, few of us will ever find ourselves in that enviable position!)

The trade association for literary agents in the United Kingdom is the Association of Authors' Agents (who can be found at 11 Jubilee Place, London SW3 3TE). All literary agents who belong to the Association are bound by its code of practice, but there are many reputable agents who do not belong to it. The *Writers' and Artists' Yearbook* – see page 32 for more about this essential reference tool for the prospective author – gives a list of more than 100 agents in the U.K. If you are thinking of employing an agent, you should always send a preliminary letter to find out whether he/she will be interested in your proposed book. Most agents specialise in particular types of material and many will not accept unsolicited manuscripts.

## Vanity publishers

Finally, before going on to consider in more detail the way to present your ideas to a potential publisher, it is worth sounding a warning note about so-called 'vanity publishers'.

You will no doubt have seen advertisements from time to time in the national press offering budding authors the opportunity to publish. Only too often these companies turn out to be offering to publish books at the author's expense. Unfortunately, so strong is the urge of some prospective writers to see themselves in print – perhaps after many rejections from reputable publishing houses – that they are prepared to pay such publishers for the privilege.

It cannot be repeated too often that if a publishing company thinks a book is worth publishing it will bear the expense of publishing it and will pay the author, either by a straight fee or by a percentage of the money it makes from sales of the book (see Chapter 5, pages 61 to 63). No reputable publishing firm will ask the author to pay for the production of his or her own book and any company which does so should be treated with the greatest suspicion.

Vanity publishers have no interest in selling books – indeed, few bookshops would be interested in stocking books they recognise as coming from such publishers, since they will generally be books that have failed to get published elsewhere. While not all may be cynically exploiting the aspirations and gullibility of prospective authors, none will help you to reach the book-buying public. At best you will have the dubious privilege of seeing your name in print. At worst you may actually damage your reputation.

As previously stated, if there is really a market for your book, and if you are really in a position to write it, you will eventually find a publisher willing to take it on and bear the expense of producing and marketing it. If, after all your efforts, you cannot find a publisher, you may have to face the fact that your book is not publishable. Paying to have the book appear may be a salve to hurt pride, but it will not achieve the real aim of getting published, which is to bring your work to the attention of a wider audience.

# 2

# Will your Idea Sell?

As we have seen, publishers are commercial creatures. They sell their products – books or other forms of information – in specialist markets and expect to make money by doing so. And in order to create those products they need to team up with authors.

Only a very small number of book publishers actually have authors on their staff to write the material they publish. The vast majority need to find authors outside the company to write books for them, and are continually on the look-out for likely candidates. If you are seriously interested in writing a book and believe you have the knowledge, ability and sheer self-discipline to do so, you are already a possible candidate. What you have to do now is decide whether the subject you have in mind will really make a marketable book and, if you believe it will, to convince a publishing house that your idea will sell.

We shall deal with the question of how to choose likely publishers, and how to submit your book proposal to them, in Chapters 3 and 4. For the moment, though, we need to consider what you want to write about and whether there is likely to be a market for it. And remember: the time to think about these things is *before* you start to write. If your aim is to get published, there is no point spending months, or even years, writing a complete book if a few days' thought at this stage would have told you that there would not be a market for it. As already mentioned in the last chapter, publishing is a business, and no commercial publisher can afford to publish a book that will not sell.

# Choosing your subject

The standard advice that has been given to generations of budding authors is to *write about what you know*. It has been said so many times that it has become something of a cliché. But like so many clichés it has a very solid basis in truth.

In fact, if you are thinking of writing a book, you probably know already what you want to write about. Few of us have enough knowledge about enough subjects for us to be able to choose freely from a wide range of areas. Most people considering launching themselves on the uncertain seas of authorship do so because they have expertise in a particular area and feel they want to communicate that expertise to other people in a form that will extend beyond their immediate sphere of influence. There is also the satisfaction of providing lasting evidence of one's knowledge. Moreover, few people are disinterested enough not to feel a certain thrill at the prospect that a book of theirs may establish itself as the standard work on its subject and may still be in print long after they are dead.

Quite often we realise towards the end of our working lives, or at the end of a distinct period in our careers, that we have accumulated a wealth of experience or knowledge in a particular field. We feel we are good at our jobs, and have successfully trained other people to be good at theirs. Why not make that knowledge available to a wider public than we shall ever be able to reach by holding in-company training courses or speaking at conferences and seminars?

Alternatively, we may have hobbies or leisure interests in which we have become exceptionally knowledgeable. Mixing with people of similar interests, we may begin to realise that we know much more about the subject or activity in question than most of the people we meet. If you are interested in windsurfing or the history of the theodolite and have found that there is nothing more you can learn from the existing books on the subject, why not think about *writing* the book you would like to read?

This is very often the way books come to be published. People realise that they would like to read a book on a particular aspect of their interests and find that there is no such book. Alternatively, there may already be a book, or even a number of books, on a particular subject, but they feel that none of them is very good or covers the subject in quite the way they think it should be covered. If *you* can't find the book you would like to read, there is a strong possibility that other people can't find it either. You may well have spotted a gap in the market. And it is precisely this sort of gap that publishers spend their time trying to fill. You may well be the person to help them do it.

## What makes books sell?

This is a question publishers are always asking themselves. Any publishing house which found the perfect answer would soon put its competitors out of business!

### The size of the market

Obviously, there is a large element of risk in publishing, just as there is in any commercial enterprise. No publisher can really be sure how a book will sell until it is actually in front of the book-buying public. But in today's business climate no commercial publisher can afford to take on a book for which the market is not broad enough to offer a reasonable likelihood of profit from sales after all the costs of production and marketing, as well as payments to authors and general overhead costs, have been met.

What 'broad enough' means will depend on the type of book, the type of people it is aimed at and the sort of price they are prepared to pay for the information it gives them. It will also depend on how easy it is to reach those people through the sales channels publishers have available to them. A highly priced specialist book on, say, the workings of the commodity futures markets, aimed at professional commodity brokers, may be considered successful if it sells 1,500 copies in two years. A management text aimed at students studying for college courses throughout the English-speaking world may sell thousands or even tens of thousands of copies a year.

### Factors which make a book successful

There are a number of factors that may make a book sell. The quality of the material, the standard of production, the author's reputation, the effectiveness of the marketing – all these considerations can have a bearing on whether or not a book succeeds.

But the most important factor of all is whether the book answers a need. However beautifully written or presented it may be, no book will sell if nobody wants to read it.

### What creates a need for a book?

Again, there are a number of different factors at work. There may simply be no book on the subject. However, since there are thousands of non-fiction books published every year, and since most publishers are specialists, continually looking for gaps in their markets and acting to fill them as they arise, it is actually quite rare for there to be no book at all in a particular subject area. Nonetheless, there are many technical areas in which the pace of change is very rapid and new developments are continually occurring. This is especially true of such fields as the applied sciences, where whole new industries have grown up around developments in biotechnology or information technology. Similarly, the world of high finance has seen extraordinary changes in recent years, with new markets and new techniques developing at an unprecedented rate. Gaps can arise too in such areas as the law, where new legislation creates a need for new information.

It is perhaps more usual for there already to be a book or books available on a subject, but for them to be inadequate in some way. This may be because they have been overtaken by events and have become outdated, or because they were not written with the real needs of their readers in mind. Alternatively, they may have been poorly marketed by the company which published them. As in many other areas of commercial life, it is not unusual for the second or third book published on a particular subject to do better than the first one. The first author will be writing without any existing texts as a guide and the publisher may have to awaken the market to its need for the book. Reviewers may point out omissions or inaccuracies. These are all things that subsequent authors and publishers can learn from and take advantage of. There is often scope for a better book, or a book with a new approach, on a subject already well represented in print.

Demand for books can also arise as a result of changes in public attitudes. An example of this is the rash of books that have appeared recently on 'green' issues. People have been writing and publishing books on environmental matters for years, but the sudden growth of public awareness about the importance of the environment, especially since the Chernobyl accident and the revelations about the erosion of the ozone layer, have created new opportunities which publishers have been quick to exploit.

Other less quantifiable needs may also prompt people to buy books. The autobiography of a public figure, or the views on management techniques of a captain of industry who is also a household name, may be bought simply because we feel a need to know how such people look at the world.

### Being sure of your market

There are many reasons, then, why people buy books or choose one book rather than another just as there are many reasons why people buy particular types of cat food. No publisher can hope to know exactly what will sell and what will not. Indeed, a publishing company which never took any risks would probably soon find itself out of business. But in order to demonstrate to a potential publisher that your idea for a book is worth considering, you will have to be able to demonstrate that it answers a need. No-one can be sure that a book will sell, even if there *is* an obvious need for it. But if there is no such need, you can be pretty sure that it won't.

In order to demonstrate that a need exists, you will have to do some preliminary market research. The rest of this chapter is about assessing the likely market for your book, looking at the competition and deciding how best to approach your subject in order to make sure that your book is the one people will buy.

## Assessing the market for your idea

Few private individuals have the facilities to mount a scientific market research campaign. Nor would most publishers expect them to. However, in order to put forward a persuasive proposal for your book (see Chapter 4), you will have to think about the following closely-related questions:

- whom are you aiming at?
- why should they want to buy your book?
- what competition exists for your book?

### Whom are you aiming at?

Perhaps the single most important factor in developing the idea for any book is to *know your reader*. One of the great distinctions between a successful author and an unsuccessful author is that the successful author knows whom he or she is writing for.

Think very carefully about this question. Ask yourself what sort of people will want to read your book. Will it, for example, be aimed mainly at general readers or is it primarily for specialists? If it is for specialists, will they be students or trainees, or will they be qualified practitioners? If it is for students or trainees, are there specific college or training courses for which the book might be useful and, if so, how many people take them each year? If, on the other hand, it is for practitioners, can you identify them by job-title or professional status? Again, can you find out roughly how many of them there are?

Think too about where these people might be. Most people will probably think first and foremost of their own country. But is this the total market? Most publishers now operate in international markets and will want to sell a book wherever there may be a need for it. How international will yours be?

## Why should they want to buy your book?
We have already looked at the sort of factors that may create a demand for a book. Now is the time to work out which of them applies to yours.

For example, have there been changes in the outside world – either actual events or changes in fashion or behaviour – which create a need for it? Is there a new or revised college course for which you want it to become required reading? Will people buy it because they want to develop a general understanding of the subject or because it will help them to do their job better?

Clearly, one of the main reasons why people will buy a new book is because it offers them something they cannot get from existing books. Closely bound up with the question 'Why should people want to buy your book?', then, is the question of what competition exists for it.

## What competition exists for your book?
It is worth researching the competition as thoroughly as you possibly can. There is no substitute for tracking down competitive books in your local library or bookshop and reading them. You may be able to tell a certain amount about them by their titles or prices or formats, but you can easily be caught out. (Chapter 3 gives more information on how to find out about similar books – see pages 32 to 33.)

### Are there other books on the subject?
Is there no other book on the subject at all? If not, is it because the potential market is too small or too inaccessible for any publisher ever to have seriously considered reaching it? Or is it – as is more likely – that you have actually spotted a gap which no publisher has noticed? After all, publishers are no more immune to overlooking the obvious than other mortals!

If there are existing books on the subject, how will yours be different or better? Look at the date of publication of the most recent editions in each case. Are they out of date? Think carefully about the markets the competitive books are aiming for. Are they different from the market you want to reach and, if so, in what respects? Are they aimed at students where yours would be aimed at professionals? Are they theoretical where yours would be practical? Remember that books with similar or even identical titles can be aimed at very different groups of people. For example, a book on bills of exchange could be directed at lawyers or at exporters or at practising bankers. A book on space flight could be written for the interested layperson or for the astronautical engineer.

Alternatively, you may find that while there are a number of publications on different aspects of your subject, there is nothing that pulls everything together in one book.

### The international market

Remember too what was said above about the increasingly international nature of publishing. Are the existing books limited to one geographical market? Will yours be relevant to, say, the United States and Great Britain, where others are written for the British market alone?

### Other forms of competition

Finally, do not overlook the fact that competition can come from types of publication or information service other than books. If you have an idea for a directory or a yearbook, for example, it would be worth checking to see whether the information you intend to include in it is already available on-line from a database publisher. Or if you want to write a book on tax matters, is there already a looseleaf information service providing updates to subscribers at regular intervals? There may still be a need for your book, but it may require answering in a different way.

# Choosing your approach

If, once you have researched the market for your book, you are still firmly convinced that there is a demand for it, you will have to give some thought to the precise approach you will be taking. There are a number of factors you will need to consider.

### Is there a book in it?

You will have to ask yourself whether there is enough material for a whole book on the aspects of the subject you have identified as being marketable. Perhaps they have not been covered in the way you propose because there simply isn't enough to be said about them to fill a whole book. If so, are there other subjects you should be adding? Or would that be to pad the book out artificially?

Alternatively, is there too much subject matter for a single book? Should you be more selective in your coverage and, if so, what should you exclude? Are there perhaps two or more books to be written where you thought originally there was only one?

### Aiming at the right level

You will have to decide too how best to present your material in order to meet the needs of the readership. Should you, for example, be taking a highly practical approach with plenty of checklists and worked examples, or should you be writing a more general analytical overview? Should you be assuming a high level of basic knowledge in your readers or will you need to go back to first principles? If your book is about a fast-changing field, how will you address the problem that it may become out of date very quickly? Will you need to include illustrations and, if so, what sort would best suit the market? Roughly how long do you think the book should be?

### The costs involved

In asking yourself all these questions you should also remember that your book must be a commercial proposition for the publishers. Publishers will not expect you to have a detailed knowledge of the economics of the book publishing business. But you should at least bear in mind that a book which costs a great deal to produce will generally have to be sold at a very high price if the publisher is to make any money on it, unless its potential market is so large that the publisher can expect to achieve significant economies of scale by printing it in very large numbers.

For example, typesetting can be very expensive, especially for technical material such as mathematical formulae. It will therefore be difficult say, to sell a very long and complicated book on statistical analysis at a cheap price unless there is a very broad potential market for it. Again, it is very expensive to include colour plates in a book. If your book depends upon having a large number of full-colour illustrations, and yet has only a fairly small specialist readership, the publisher will probably have to sell it at a very high price in order to make a profit. Is this realistic for the sort of reader you have in mind?

### Are you up to the job ?
Finally, it is worth asking yourself at this stage whether you really know enough about the subject to write a book on it and, if you do, whether you are confident about your ability to communicate that knowledge. You will inevitably know more about some parts of the subject than others. Are you sure you can find the information you need to write meaningfully about the things you currently know least about? Will you need specialist advice on any aspects of the subject and, if so, do you know where to go for it? Now is the time to be brutally honest with yourself on these points. There is no sense in persuading a publisher to take you on as an author only to find that you cannot fulfil your contract.

We shall have more to say about the way to convert your market research into a proposal for potential publishers in Chapter 4. But first we must identify those potential publishers. How should you go about finding the best people to approach with your idea? This is the subject of Chapter 3.

# 3

# Choosing your Publisher

As we have already seen, not all publishers publish books of all kinds. Most specialise in a particular type of publishing, which normally means that they specialise in one or more subject areas and/or one or more types of reader.

One of the commonest mistakes made by aspiring authors is to send their proposal to the wrong kind of publisher. There is absolutely no point in sending a proposal for a book on gardening to a publisher who specialises in books on cookery, or one for a book on computer science to a publisher who specialises in books on accountancy. The proposal will simply be returned with a short letter of rejection. It is a waste of everyone's time, not to mention the postage cost.

It is therefore crucial to research the types of publisher who deal with the kind of book you are proposing to write. You should aim to draw up a list of such publishers and, as far as possible, to put them in order of preference, so that you can send your proposal to them, starting with the one at the top of the list and working down until – you hope – one of them accepts it for publication.

How should you go about compiling this list? How can you find information about potential publishers and what sort of information should you be looking for?

# Sources of information about publishers

### The Writers' and Artists' Yearbook
By far the most widely used published source of information about publishers in the U.K. is the *Writers' and Artists' Yearbook,* which is published annually by A. & C. Black (Publishers) Ltd. of London. The book lists all the major and many of the minor book publishers in the U.K., and also includes sections on Australia, Canada, India, Ireland, New Zealand, South Africa, the United States and some Commonwealth countries. Each entry gives the address, telephone number and date of foundation of the company concerned, together with a list of its directors. More importantly, it gives a list of the main subject areas in which that company publishes. In addition to its directory listings, the *Yearbook* also includes a number of useful articles on different aspects of the writing and publishing process. It is well worth getting hold of a copy.

### Other sources of information
Invaluable companion though it is, the *Yearbook* gives only a bald listing of the professional interests of the publishers it includes. In researching the sort of publishers you ought to approach, there is no substitute for looking at as many books as you can find on your subject or other similar subjects and noting down which publishers produce which kind.

A good place to start is your own bookshelves. Follow this up with visits to good bookshops (particularly those which specialise in the kind of book you have in mind) and to your local libraries. If the library has a subject catalogue, look through every section in it that has a bearing on your idea and make a note of the titles listed. Locate the books on the shelves and pore over each of them until you have a feel for the kind of angle they take, the kind of readership they are aimed at and the kind of format the publishers have adopted (e.g. hardback or paperback, illustrated or non-illustrated). Above all, write down the names of all the publishers represented, list under each name the books you have seen published by them and note the kind of approach they took. Indicate the books which took the approach most similar to the one you yourself have in mind. Check the published price of these books in a bookshop if you can. Then find out the addresses of their publishers from the *Writers' and Artists' Yearbook*.

All publishers produce catalogues of the books they publish and of their forthcoming titles. Telephone the publishers which produce the sort of book you have in mind and ask them to send you a copy of their latest catalogue. (The switchboard will generally be able to put you through to the right people; if they can't, ask for the sales manager.) The larger publishers may produce separate catalogues for their different subject areas.

## What to look for in a potential publisher

The best publisher for your book is the publisher who will be able to sell it most effectively. This will not necessarily be the publisher who produces the most beautiful-looking books on the subject or the publisher whose name is most familiar to you. Nor will it necessarily be the biggest publisher in the field. But it will almost certainly be one of the publishers who produce the most books with the greatest similarity to the one you want to write.

In other words, what you should be looking for in a potential publisher is expertise in producing books on your subject and in selling them to the sort of people you want to reach. The more specialist your idea, the easier it will be to identify likely candidates. But however specialist it is, the main questions you should ask yourself about any publisher are:

- do they have an established list in this subject area?
- are the books on that list aimed at your potential readership?

The catalogues you receive from the publishers you have contacted will be the best way of answering these questions. Read them carefully. Take particular note of the target markets identified in the descriptions of the books. Are they, for example, generally books for students and academics, or are they for professionals? Are they for the general reader or for the specialist? Are they priced at a level your own target readership could afford?

You may be able to glean further information – or at least further impressions – from local booksellers or librarians or from anyone you know who has a specialist interest in the area you want to write about. But basically you have now used all the most helpful channels open to you. Once you have asked yourself these questions and found the answers to them, you are in a position to draw up your list of likely publishers. The next question is: How should you approach them?

## Making your initial approach

Before we look at the detail of the initial approach (which is the subject of Chapter 4), it is worth considering the basic rules about contacting publishers. There are two things to remember:

● always write

● always send a proposal, not a complete manuscript

### *Always write*

Do not turn up on the publisher's doorstep and expect to be able to discuss your idea in person. You will almost certainly be turned away at the reception desk and even if you are not, you will make a very unprofessional impression.

It could well be worth telephoning in advance of sending your proposal to find out the best person to send it to in the company, but it is possible that the switchboard will not be able to tell you on the basis of the kind of information you can give over the telephone. The right person will normally be the commissioning editor of the list of which your book might form a part. The publisher's catalogue may give the name of the individual, but if in doubt, address your proposal to the editorial director.

Anything you send to the publisher must be typed or word-processed. When publishers say 'manuscript' they *always* mean typescript or word-processed copy. Handwritten proposals will very rarely be taken seriously.

It is generally best to send your proposal to one publisher at a time. If you are sending it to a number of publishers at once, you should say so in your covering letter. Do not send a photocopied covering letter. Preferably send a top copy of your proposal. If for some reason you can't, send a photocopy. Never send a carbon copy. Always keep a copy of anything you send, and always enclose a stamped self-addressed envelope of sufficient size and value to accommodate your proposal if you want it back in the event of the publisher rejecting it. Not all publishers will use your envelope if they need to return the material, but some – especially the smaller presses – will not be happy about bearing the return postage if no such envelope is enclosed.

Any reputable publisher will keep your proposal confidential. You need not worry that they will rush off with your idea and find someone else to write it. No publisher who did so would stay in business for long.

### Always send a proposal, never a complete manuscript

It cannot be stressed too often that all publishers prefer to receive a proposal for a book rather than a completed manuscript. If you follow the approach suggested in this book, you will put together a proposal before you begin the business of writing. But even if you have already completed your manuscript you should send a proposal of the kind outlined in Chapter 4. You might mention in your covering letter that the completed manuscript is available, should the publisher wish to see it, but wait until you have received an expression of interest before sending the whole thing off.

So what form should your proposal take? It is time to look at this question in more detail.

# 4

# Submitting your Proposal

We have now seen something of the way publishers operate and of the factors that may determine whether or not a book will sell. By now you will have measured your idea against these factors and made an assessment of its marketability. In the process your original idea may have undergone a certain amount of transformation and you may have a clearer view of the sort of book a potential publisher might be interested in. You will also have established which publishers produce the kind of book you want to publish.

You have now arrived at the most crucial stage of the whole process of trying to get published. It is time to put together the package of material with which to approach your first choice of publisher.

It is important to remember that at this stage you are effectively a salesperson for your own idea. You have to sell your idea to the publisher by presenting it in the way most likely to attract the publisher's attention and to make him or her consider it seriously as a possible publication. Remember too that you will be competing for consideration not only with other unsolicited proposals that may cross the publisher's desk but also with proposals submitted by potential authors whom the publisher has approached.

Although these solicited proposals are very unlikely to be on exactly the same subject as your own, they will have certain advantages over yours when it comes to capturing the publisher's attention and being taken seriously. For one thing, the publisher will be waiting for them to arrive and will also be pretty confident that the ideas themselves are sound, since they will generally be the publisher's own. Also, the potential author in each case will probably be known to the commissioning editor, who will normally have met him or her by this stage. And – perhaps most important of all – he or she will have been given a very clear idea of what the publishing company is looking for in a proposal.

It is obviously in your interests to minimise these advantages as far as you can. In other words, you will have to make very sure that your proposal looks as professional, and meets the publisher's requirements for a package of this kind as fully, as those the commissioning editor has sought out. Let us therefore turn to the question of what publishers are looking for when they receive a proposal for a future publication.

## What do publishers look for in a proposal?

The main thing publishers need to glean from a book proposal is whether or not the idea it contains can be developed into a saleable book. They will basically want to know what the book will contain, whom it will be aimed at, why you feel there is a need for it and why you think you are the person to write it. Your proposal should clearly communicate the answers to these questions.

### *Aim for clarity*
Always remember that, while you will have been thinking about your book for a long time and will be thoroughly familiar with what you want to say, how you want to say it and whom you want to say it to, the publisher will be encountering it for the first time. Make sure that you are not taking anything for granted. The closer you are to the detail of a subject, the easier it is to overlook the obvious. For example, the contents page of the book you are now reading, which is very similar to the synopsis originally submitted to the publishers, gives no clues to the fact that it covers only the

publishing of works of non-fiction. This had to be spelt out elsewhere in the proposal. You should not assume that the commissioning editor is a complete novice, but you should not assume that he or she is clairvoyant either.

At the same time, the commissioning editor will not necessarily be an expert in your field, even if he or she deals mainly with books on similar subjects. It is quite possible for him or her to have a firm grasp of the subject area, and to be able to deal meaningfully with experts in that area, without knowing all the nuts and bolts as they (or you) do. You will probably not be going into sufficient detail at the proposal stage for this to cause any difficulties, but it is worth remembering in your later discussions.

### *Do not include any unnecessary information in your proposal*
Always bear in mind the questions the publisher is likely to ask and concentrate on answering them as fully as you can without swamping the publisher with detail. For example, he or she will not be interested in your complete life story or a lengthy exposition of how the idea for the book first came to you. Too much detail here will actually obscure the reasons why you should write the book and why you feel there is a need for it.

Do not prescribe what you think should be the print -run or price of the book or suggest how you think it ought to be marketed. Publishers do not like to be told how to do their job any more than other professionals. If the book is very different from the kind of book they normally produce, you are probably approaching the wrong publisher. If it *is* the kind of book they normally publish, they will know how to produce and market it already. There are obviously exceptions to this rule – there may, for example, be important reasons for not marketing a particular book in a particular country, and it would be a great help to the publisher if you were to mention these in your proposal – but by and large it is worth observing it. You can always make suggestions of this kind at a later stage when you have met the commissioning editor and established your credibility.

It is also unnecessary to try to make your proposal look like pages from a finished book. Publishers are used to dealing with typescripts and may feel you are forcing the pace a little if you present them with something intended to mimic a published book. It is rare, even with desktop publishing systems, for private individuals to be able to match the typesetting and printing standards publishers will be used to achieving and there is therefore a danger, ironic as this may seem, of looking amateurish by trying to look more professional than the occasion demands.

Finally, there is no need to send any sample material at this stage of the process. If the publishers want to see such material they will ask for a draft chapter or two later. Your initial proposal should aim to convince them that this is what they *do* want.

## What form should your proposal take?

Bearing in mind what has been said about the things publishers need to know from a proposal, it is now worth looking in a little more detail at what form such a proposal should take.

At this stage of the process publishers will not want to be inundated with paper. They will want to be told no more and no less than will enable them to decide whether it is worthwhile taking your idea further. If they decide it is, they will probably want to meet you to discuss the project in more detail and may well ask you to expand certain areas of your proposal or, as mentioned above, provide sample material for them to look at. For the time being, a package of up to half a dozen sheets of A4 typescript will generally be quite sufficient.

The basic elements of this package should be:

- a synopsis of the book's contents

- a résumé of the *kind* of book you have in mind

- a covering letter

Let us look at what each of these should include.

# The synopsis

The synopsis is the skeleton of the book. Your intention in drafting it should be to give the publishers the clearest possible idea of the shape the finished book will take. What you should therefore be aiming to produce is a document rather like a more detailed version of the contents pages which are printed at the beginning of a published book.

## Structuring the synopsis

Your synopsis should be divided into chapters, as the finished work will be, and should give an indication of the subject areas to be covered in each chapter. Since the text in most works of non-fiction is divided up by different levels of heading, it is a good idea to divide up your proposed chapters in the same way. Just as a logical hierarchy of headings in a printed book gives the reader a series of pointers to the structure of what he or she is reading, so a series of headings within the proposed chapters of your synopsis will give the publisher a clearer idea of the structure of those chapters than a mere paragraph or two of connected text. (This may not be possible, of course, with all kinds of book.)

## Deciding what to include in the synopsis

Quite apart from telling potential publishers what your book will look like, producing a synopsis of this kind is a very useful exercise in disciplined thinking. Few subjects are completely self-contained or organise themselves naturally in a single definitive way. Most interconnect with other subjects at many points and can be treated in many different ways. As you sit down to think about what your book will actually cover, you will find yourself having to make difficult decisions about these matters at every turn. It may sound obvious to say that you will have to decide what to leave in, what to leave out and how to deal with the things you decide to leave in, but in practice this can be far from easy.

Even a relatively short book on a relatively accessible subject is a minefield of these sorts of decision. For example, if you are writing a book about the great fenland floods of 1947, you will need to decide how much you want to say about previous floods. If you say nothing at all, it will be difficult for the reader to measure how disastrous the 1947 floods really were; if you say too much, you will be starting to write a more general book about flooding. Again, you will have to decide how much to say about the climatic conditions which produced the floods. You are not writing a meteorological study, but unless you give some scientific background your readers will not understand how the floods came to happen. Again, should you start your story with the terrible winter of 1946-47 or with the formation of the fenland in prehistory? And should you finish it with the harvest that followed the fenland floods or with the great engineering works of the 1960s which were a direct result of the 1947 disaster?

## The value of a good synopsis

A good logical synopsis is an excellent way of making these sorts of decision at an early stage of the process. Indeed, many authors say that producing a synopsis is actually a very large part of the work involved in writing a complete book. It is a crucial opportunity to impose a structure on the shapeless mass of material from which you will need to chisel out your book. It is also an opportunity to persuade potential publishers – and perhaps yourself too! – that you are capable of the degree of logical thought required for the task of authorship.

Of course, publishers know, as you do, that the final book is bound not to follow this synopsis precisely. The details of the structure will almost certainly change in some way or other during the course of the writing. But within reason, this will not matter. The synopsis is a way of showing that you have thought about your book as a whole and in its constituent parts, and that it adds up to a publishable proposition. It will also provide a crucial scaffolding for you when you start to build the book itself.

We shall have a more detailed look at the business of drafting the synopsis later in this chapter (see page 50). But first it is time to consider the second plank of your proposal.

## The résumé

Your synopsis will give the potential publisher a clear idea of what you are intending to cover in your book. But, as we have seen, there are a number of other things publishers need to know about a proposed book before they are in a position to decide whether or not it is worth pursuing, and a synopsis alone will not necessarily deal with these. Between them, the résumé and your covering letter should give the publisher all the rest of the information he or she requires.

The length of the résumé will depend to some extent on the complexity of the book you are proposing. Generally, though, a piece of prose of about 300 to 500 words should be sufficient. The main points you should aim to cover are:

- the market for the book
- the general approach you will be taking
- the likely length of the book
- a rough idea of any timescale you have in mind for writing it
- your qualifications for writing it.

Let us look at each of these in turn.

### The market for the book

In order to convince potential publishers that your book is worth considering, you are going to have to convince them that there is a market for it. Once you have succeeded in this, you will have won half the battle.

You may have produced a weak synopsis, but if you have made a strong case that there is a market for a book in the area you want to cover, a publisher will almost certainly be prepared to work with you to polish the synopsis until it forms the basis for that book. If, on the other hand, your synopsis is a paragon of logic and clarity but you have not been able to convince the publisher that your book will sell, you are unlikely to get a positive response.

So – your proposal should aim to convey to the publisher the answers to the three questions we looked at in Chapter 2 when assessing the market for your book, namely:

● whom are you aiming at?

● why should they want to buy the book?

● what competition exists for your book?

### Identify the readership

This is your opportunity to demonstrate that you know your reader. Identify your target readership as precisely as possible, giving such details as job-titles and likely numbers if you can. If it will be useful to specific training or college courses, specify which ones and, if you can, how many people study for them each year.

Remember too that the publisher will want to know how international your book will be in its appeal. If it will be equally useful to the category of readers you have identified for it regardless of whether they live in Scotland, the United States or Australia, then say so in your résumé. If, on the other hand, there are particular English-speaking territories to which it will not be relevant – for example because of differences in legal or regulatory régimes – identify these too.

Do not try to suggest that the market for your book is wider than it really is. A publisher will always be more interested in a book with a clearly defined target market (assuming of course that this market is large enough to make it a commercial proposition) than in a book which, in trying to hit a number of targets, becomes so unfocussed in its approach that it misses them all. It is almost as useful for the publisher to know who will *not* be interested in the book as it is to know who will.

### Demonstrate the need for your book

The résumé is also the place to convince the publisher that people will want to buy your book. If there have been specific changes in the external world which have created a need for the book you are proposing, you should outline these. For example, if you are writing a book about investing in stocks and shares, it would be helpful to sketch in any changes in the pattern of share ownership which make you feel there is a need for new information on the subject. Again, if you are writing a book on the role of the reindeer in the economic life of the Laplanders, it would be a good idea to mention how much more topical this subject has become in the aftermath of the Chernobyl accident.

Alternatively, if there have been no remarkable changes in the outside world but you have spotted a particular pattern of behaviour that you think will sustain the market for a book, say so and back your claim up with statistics if you have them available. For example, if you were proposing to write a book of walks in and around Cambridge or Stratford-upon-Avon, it would be worth pointing out how high these centres rank in the list of towns visited by foreign tourists in the U.K.

Similarly, if your book is geared to a new examination syllabus or to a revised college curriculum, do not assume that the publisher will necessarily know of these changes. Give a brief explanation of the effect they have had and of how your proposed book meets the new need they have created.

Do not overlook the fact that you may have at your disposal a fairly persuasive argument for the need for the book simply by being the person you are. If you are a professional person writing a book for other practitioners in your own field of work, for example, you are likely to be exactly the sort of person who would buy the book you are proposing. You are bound to be somewhat biased, of course – and anecdotal evidence about the number of your colleagues who have said they would buy the book if it were published is not likely to be any more scientific – but you are nonetheless peculiarly well placed to know the needs of the market you are aiming at, and a potential publisher will certainly note this. There is more on what you should say about yourself in your proposal later in this chapter (see pages 48 to 49).

### Describe the competition

You should also outline the competition for the book in this part of your proposal. This will not only help to establish the need for your proposed book; it will also impress the potential publisher with your market awareness and the commercial realism of your approach.

Obviously, the strongest card you will have to play is that there is no other book on the subject you are proposing. Since, as was mentioned in Chapter 2, this will rarely be the case, you should be very sure of your ground before making such a claim. However, if after all your hard research you are confident that yours *will* be the only book on the subject, it is a claim to be made loud and clear.

As we have seen, however, it is more probable that there are already competitive books on your subject. If so, the crucial requirement is to give a reasoned and sustainable analysis of the ways in which your book will differ from them or will do what they do better. Sell the strengths of your book as hard as you can. If the existing books are out of date, say so. If you have found errors, oversights or incorrect emphases in a competitive book, or have seen reviews pointing these things out, say this too and explain how your book will avoid falling into the same traps. Alternatively, if you are aiming to bring together in a single volume information which has previously been available only from disparate sources, do not be shy of making this claim.

Be very specific about differences between the markets the competitive books are aiming at and the ones you intend to reach. For example, if all the books on your subject are aimed primarily at students and yours will be aimed primarily at professionals, or if yours will be more international in its coverage than the competing books, make sure you point this out.

**The general approach**

In outlining the target market for your book you will have given potential publishers the most important information they will be seeking from your proposal. In your synopsis you will have given them a clear idea of the overall structure and content of the book. Now it is time to draw the two together and explain how the way in which you will be writing the book will make it especially appropriate to the market you have identified.

This explanation need not be particularly lengthy. It simply needs to add a little flesh to the skeleton of the synopsis and perhaps draw particular attention to any features of that skeleton which are especially important in the light of the book's market. For example, to revert to our book of walks around Stratford -upon-Avon, you might want to point out that most of the walks are circular, or that they all include picnic spots, or that they are graded according to their level of difficulty for young children. Again, if you were writing a book on financial accounting for managers without financial training, you might want to point out that only basic numeracy will be required in order to understand what you have to say, because you will be taking the reader through the subject from first principles. Conversely, if you expect the reader of your manual of production engineering techniques to have a high level of technical knowledge, it would be wise to say so in your résumé.

This is also the place to mention any features of the proposed book which may have an impact upon the marketing or production of the finished work. For example, will you be including line drawings or graphs? Does the book require black and white photographs or colour plates? If it is a student text, will it incorporate sample examination questions and answers?

Again, try to step back from your proposal and see it with the eyes of the publisher looking at it for the first time. It may be patently obvious to you that, say, your book of walks must include maps of the routes, but it is as well to spell this out and indicate the types of map you are planning to use. This kind of thing is an essential component of the overall approach and can also make a significant difference to the cost of the whole project. In Great Britain, for example, the Ordnance Survey have a virtual monopoly on maps and charge royalties for reproduction.

## How long will your book be?

Publishers think of books in terms of numbers of words. You will find when you come to write your book that authors soon have to start thinking in this way too. So now is a good time to start!

Since typesetting is a significant part of the cost of producing a book, potential publishers will be keen to form an idea of the likely length an author expects his or her book to run to. At this early stage of the process, such an idea will necessarily be something of a stab in the dark, but it will at least indicate whether you are thinking of something the length of the Highway Code or of the London telephone directory.

There is no such animal as a typical book and therefore no such thing as a typical length. The 'right' length for any given work will depend entirely on the sort of considerations we have been looking at in this chapter – namely, what you have to say, how you are going to say it and whom you are going to say it to.

Your synopsis is the best place to start when trying to estimate the likely length of your book. You will want to ensure that the internal balance of the book reflects the relative importance of the different subjects you are covering. If you have broken your synopsis down into its component parts in the way suggested in this chapter, you should be able to estimate the likely length of each subsection in relation to its neighbours and to build up from this an estimate of the length of the whole book.

## How long will it take you to write the book?

This is probably the least important information to include in your résumé. If you have had no prior experience of writing books, you will probably find it very difficult to make a meaningful guess at how long it will take.

If you have specific reasons for thinking that the book would do better if produced at one particular time rather than at another – for example, if a new series of regulations is about to come into force in the field you are writing about, or if there is an important anniversary in the offing – it would be worth saying so in your proposal. If not, it would be better to give no indication of your likely timescale than to give one that turns out to be hopelessly adrift.

## Why you?

If you have never written a book before, you may wonder whether publishers will ever take you seriously as a potential author, however good your idea. They will.

Remember that there are relatively few professional authors. Most non-fiction books of the kind we are considering are written by people who are experts in their subject first and writers second. In some cases, authors may not even be established experts. They may simply be intelligent generalists with a gift for researching and assimilating information and presenting it in a lucid and appropriate form to their readers. After all, many works of non-fiction are aimed at general readers, and the general writer is in some ways the best person to know their needs. And we have all come across experts who have no idea how to make their specialism intelligible to the uninitiated.

If you have spotted a gap in the market and have put together a strong proposal for a book to fill it, you will probably already know a fair amount about the subject in question. Some of your qualifications for writing about it may well have come over in your discussion of the need for the book, since it is likely that you will have recognised this need as a result of knowledge gained in your professional or private life.

In outlining the reasons why you feel you are able to write the book, concentrate only on those qualifications that are directly relevant to the subject and your approach. These may be such experiences as running training courses or speaking at conferences and seminars; academic qualifications in the areas concerned; or practical experience of the activities the book describes. If you hold any official positions relating to the subject matter of the book, it would be worth mentioning them. If you have written articles on the subject in your professional or trade journal, you might consider enclosing photocopies of them. If not, the publisher will be able to judge something of your capacity to write from your résumé. There is no point mentioning your essay prizes at school or college. The main thing is to establish your credibility as someone who knows the subject, not as someone who can match the style of Dickens or Jane Austen.

## The covering letter

Like most covering letters, this one is probably best kept short. There is little point repeating what you have said in your résumé of the book, but it may be worth summarising its main points in a short paragraph just to give the publisher an immediate idea of what is to come. You may also prefer to say what you have to say about yourself in the letter rather than in the résumé.

It would be worth placing your proposed title for the book prominently below the 'Dear ___' line (see below, page 54, for more about choosing your title). This will not only draw attention to a significant part of the idea you are trying to sell, but will also help the publisher to file the proposal in-house. Some such formula as 'PROPOSED BOOK:' followed by your suggested title would be fine. Go on to explain what you are enclosing – together with such brief details of the project itself as you feel would be appropriate – and say that you look forward to hearing the publisher's views in due course. Perhaps add that you would be happy to discuss the project in further detail if the publisher wishes to do so.

Like the rest of your proposal, your covering letter should be typed or word-processed and you should include a stamped self-addressed envelope of sufficient size and value to accommodate the proposal package should you want this returned to you in the event of its rejection. As mentioned in Chapter 3, it would be best to send the letter to the editorial director if you are unsure of the name of the person in the company who will deal with it. If you have telephoned the switchboard and been given the name of someone you are sure is the right individual for the book, address it to him or her in person.

## How to draw up a synopsis

Now that we have looked at the various components of the proposal, let us go back for a moment to the first of those components – the synopsis. As has already been said, getting the synopsis right is one of the most important parts of the whole process of writing a book, and it is therefore worth looking in a little more detail at how to go about drawing it up.

Writing a synopsis is rather like writing a book in miniature. Both involve making order out of chaos. However clear the idea of the book in your mind, you will almost certainly find that it changes in significant ways as you begin to impose a logical structure on the mass of subjects you feel it should cover. The first thing to decide is what that logical structure should look like.

### *The chapter breakdown*

As has already been said, the synopsis should be divided into chapters and these should in turn be divided into their constituent parts by the use of headings and subheadings. Each chapter should be as self-contained as possible and should stand in a logical relation to all the other chapters. In particular, ensure that the order of the chapters makes sense. While readers of non-fiction books will not necessarily read straight through from Chapter 1 to the end, it is nonetheless irritating to come across things in Chapter 3 which you have to read Chapter 4 to understand. (This may sound very obvious, but it is surprisingly easy to overlook this kind of anomaly. It may also be impossible to eradicate it altogether. If so, you will have to rely on extensive cross-referencing when you come to write the text – see page 90.) Give each of the chapters a clear and concise title which reflects its scope. Publishers refer to these titles as chapter-headings.

## *The level of headings*

Give careful thought to the heading structure you want to use within each chapter. In doing so, you might find it helpful to look at other books on similar subjects to see how the authors have arranged their own material. Headings provide the reader with an essential guide to the structure of the book, and it is essential that whatever system you use should be as logical and consistent as possible. You should think in terms of a hierarchy of headings, along the following lines:

Chapter heading

Main heading

  Subheading

    Sub-subheadings

  Subheading

    Sub-subheadings

Main heading

  Subheading

    Sub-subheadings

etc.

Not all books will require all these levels of heading, and within a single book not all main headings will require subheadings or all subheadings require sub-subheadings. The demands of the material will determine what is appropriate in your individual case. The most complicated chapters will probably determine how many levels of heading you will need for the book as a whole. The number of headings you need at each level in any given chapter will be determined by the scope and length of the chapter concerned.

Make sure that your main headings divide each chapter up into its main subject areas and that the subheadings under each main heading are genuinely the main constituent parts of each of those areas. Make sure, too, that all the subheadings under any given main heading, or all the sub-subheadings under any given subheading, refer to subjects which have the same degree of importance as one another. (All these considerations will naturally be equally important when you come to write the book itself – see Chapter 7, page 92.)

### Balance

As far as possible without artificiality, try to make the chapters of roughly even length. While there is no hard and fast rule about this, it is a good idea to retain as much internal balance as possible. Also, if some chapters are only two or three pages long while others are 50 or 60, readers may begin to wonder whether the main determining factor is not how important the various subjects are but how much you actually know about them!

### The initial draft

You should bear in mind the suggestions described above in imposing a logical structure upon the material you want to cover in your book. You know the kinds of framework available. Now you have to decide which kind is appropriate to your needs. How should you go about it?

Probably the best way to start drafting a synopsis is simply to jot down on a blank sheet of paper the various ideas you want to cover in your book. Do this as they occur to you, in no particular order. It is a good idea to keep reading other books on aspects of your subject at this time, since they will almost certainly stimulate your thoughts as to what should be included in yours. One idea will spark off another and you will soon find natural patterns starting to emerge from your random jottings.

## Sorting the information

Group together those subjects which seem to have a natural connection with one another and try to establish the most important groupings with a view to using them as the main chapter headings. Think of the chapters as pigeon-holes in which to file all the points you want to make. If you have chosen the right labels for the pigeon-holes, it will be relatively easy to decide which points should be filed in each. Most will fit neatly into one or another hole. Some may fit in one of two or more holes and you will have to decide which is most appropriate, bearing in mind the balance and sequence of the book's parts.

Once you have done this, you can look at each chapter as a unit, sorting out from the various points you have filed in it the ones which are most important, the order in which you want to cover them, and the main items you want to include as you deal with each of them. By the end of this process you should have got your chapter headings, most of your main headings and most of your various levels of subheading.

## Refining the synopsis

It is probably worth putting the synopsis aside for a few days while you continue to read and think around your subject. Refinements will no doubt occur to you during this time. You will notice things you should have included but haven't, and things you have included which do not really fall within the scope of the book. You may spot areas of overlap between chapters. You will realise that some subjects could be better dealt with in different ways or in a different order. When you have done your fine tuning and are confident that the synopsis gives the most accurate impression possible at this juncture, you are almost ready to launch it into the unknown.

Before you do so, however, there is one final and rather important matter to be considered, and that is the title of your proposed book.

# Choosing a title

It may seem perverse to leave until last so prominent a feature of your proposed book as its title, but this is in fact a very good time to consider it. You may well have started out with an idea for a title but it is really only when you have drafted a synopsis that you will know precisely what your book will cover. If you had a good idea for a title right at the outset, you may test it against the synopsis and find that it is still exactly right. Alternatively, you may find that you ought to think again.

How important is a title? There is no doubt that a title *is* important at the proposal stage, but it is nothing like as important as it will be later on when the publisher starts to sell your book. It is also not as important as making a good case for the market for your book or producing a really first-rate synopsis. A poorly constructed book which nobody wants to buy will not become a bestseller just because it has a snappy title. Conversely, if the publishers think your idea has potential as a saleable book, they are not going to reject it just because the title you have suggested is weak. Most publishers give a great deal of thought to the titles of their books, often at quite a late stage, and as the people who have to sell the book, they will want the final say.

For the time being, then, the title is one of the means you have at your disposal to help sell your idea to the publisher, but it is not the most important one. In choosing it, you should bear in mind not only the subject of the book but also the people it is aimed at and the sort of approach you will be taking. There is no point trying to make a heavyweight book on welding techniques sound like a popular guide for the person in the street. If there is a general rule, it is to keep the main title as concise as you can without giving a false impression of the book's scope. A short title is more easily catalogued and remembered. The final title will probably also have to be short, or capable of being shortened enough to appear at the top of every other page of the printed book in what are known as 'running heads'. Remember that you can always expand on the coverage, treatment and market for the book in a longer subtitle.

# 5

# From Proposal to Contract

Your proposal is now in the hands of the publisher. What next? Most publishers receive a great many unsolicited proposals, all of which need to be considered on their merits. Most will also be busy approaching potential authors themselves, going to conferences in their subject areas, reading manuscripts already received and doing numerous administrative jobs relating to the publishing process. It may therefore be some time before you receive a reply.

It would be politic to resist becoming impatient for as long as you reasonably can. There is no need to phone up two or three days after sending your material to check that it has arrived, unless you have good reason for fearing that it may have gone astray. It would certainly be unwise to start chasing for a reply two or three weeks later. It can easily take a month or two for a publisher to respond to a proposal of this kind. It may need to be read by more than one person in the company. Alternatively, the publishing decision-makers may have regular meetings to discuss new proposals and yours may be held over with others until the next such forum. A delay may mean that the idea is being taken very seriously. Unfortunately, it is just as likely to mean that the publishers have not yet got round to looking at it.

If you have still heard nothing after a couple of months, it would be perfectly reasonable to send a polite chasing letter. If you still hear nothing, it may be time to push a little harder.

# If at first you don't succeed...

As has already been said, it is a hard truth that the road to publication is littered with rejections. If, when it does arrive, your letter from the publishers is negative, do not be dispirited. If every budding author gave up at the first hurdle, many of the names familiar to us from the bookshelves today would never have found their way into print.

Publishers may have a number of reasons for rejecting a book other than its poor quality or unmarketability. For example, they may just have commissioned a book on the same or a similar subject, or they may have taken a policy decision not to publish any more books of the kind you are proposing. They may recognise that there is a market for the book, but do not feel able to reach it effectively themselves. Most publishers will give some reason for their decision in a rejection letter, and some make a point of suggesting other publishers you might try if they feel the book has genuine potential.

If the first publisher you try does suggest someone else who may be interested, it is probably worth following up that lead next. If not, work down the list of potential publishers you have drawn up (see Chapter 3). Above all, don't despair. That said, if you still find that no-one is prepared to take the book on after you have approached every publisher on your list, you should ask yourself whether there really is a market for it in its present form. You may simply have to face up to the fact that there isn't.

## Initial discussions with the publisher

If, on the other hand, the letter you receive says that the publishers are interested in your idea in principle, what should you expect to happen next?

### The first meeting
The most likely event is that the publisher's commissioning editor will ask to meet you, either at the publishing house's offices or at

your home or business address, to discuss the proposal in further detail. Such a meeting will give you a better feel for the way the company operates and the sort of things it is looking for in its books and authors than you will have been able to get from other sources. It will also give you an opportunity to ask any questions you may have about the publishing process and the way in which a book such as yours might fit into it.

The main purpose of the meeting from the commissioning editor's point of view will be to get a clearer impression of the way you see the book and its potential market and to talk to you about any ways in which he/she feels it needs to be reshaped to meet the requirements of that market. You should take such suggestions very seriously. As mentioned earlier, the commissioning editor will not necessarily know your subject area as well as you do, but he/she will generally have a very good understanding of the way the book market works in that area and therefore of the likely needs of the book's potential readers. This is not to say that you should necessarily agree with all the commissioning editor's suggestions, but it does mean that you should consider them all as objectively as you can and should have very strong reasons for ignoring those you disagree with.

### Additional material

The likely upshot of this first meeting is that you will be asked to provide some sample material. The purpose of this request is to enable the publisher to form a more reliable impression of your style, approach and sheer ability to communicate your ideas than will generally have been possible from the proposal package. He/she may ask you to write specific sections from your proposed synopsis or, more likely, will leave the choice of material up to you. You may also be asked to come up with a revised synopsis.

Make sure that by the time you leave the meeting you have a very clear idea of what is required of you. In particular, find out roughly how many words the commissioning editor would like to see and whether he/she has any preferences as to which parts of the proposed book they come from. Find out, too, when he/she would ideally like to see them, and ensure that any date by which you promise to send them is realistic: it would be foolish to risk getting a reputation for unreliability at so early a stage.

It is possible that the package you have already sent is so thoroughly convincing, or that you are so well known in your field, that you will not be asked to provide any written samples. If so, you can expect to be given or sent a copy of the publisher's standard agreement for you to consider (see pages 61 to 69 for more about this). You will also probably be asked to give some further thought to the likely timescale for writing the book.

### Make notes of any meetings

Whatever the outcome, it is advisable in this as in any other important meeting to make clear notes about what is said and asked of you. This is not to suggest that the publishers are likely to prove unreliable or untrustworthy. Far from it. But you will be dealing with an area of commercial life that is almost certainly unfamiliar to you, and it is therefore even more important than usual to be sure you have a complete record of your discussions. Details such as the likely print-run or published price, or the way in which the publisher markets books overseas, are easily forgotten or confused and it is worth jotting them down. It is also a good way of ensuring that you really do know what is expected of you. It is much better to ask questions now than to have to phone up later.

### The relationship between author and editor

One final point before we go on to consider the writing of the sample material itself: remember that the relationship between author and commissioning editor is at the very heart of the publishing process. If your book is accepted for publication, the person you have just met will almost certainly play a crucial role in working with you to shape its development, both during the writing and after you have delivered your manuscript. Indeed, a good commissioning editor will become as committed to the success of your book as you are and will feel almost as intimate a relationship with the material. It is worth conducting your side of any initial meeting with these considerations firmly in mind.

## The sample material

Assuming the commissioning editor has not specified the sections of the book he/she would like to see, what should you aim to present?

### *What sample material should you present ?*

Generally, a chapter or two – say, about 5,000 words – will give the publishers enough to go on. There will normally be no requirement to submit the first chapters. Indeed, it is probably best not to, since these are likely to be the most introductory and therefore the least illustrative of the book as a whole. Again, there is no need for the material you submit to be consecutive. Since the publishers are hoping to form as accurate a general impression of the book as they can, it is probably best to write sections from different parts of the synopsis.

It would obviously be a good idea to cover those aspects of the subject you know best in this sample material, not least because you will want to return to the publishers as soon as you can and such sections are likely to need the least research time. You are still trying to sell your idea to the publisher and it is worth putting a lot of effort into this part of the process. Write as if every word will be pored over, because it probably will be. At the same time, make sure you strike while the iron is hot. If your initial meeting has enthused you, it will almost certainly have enthused the commissioning editor too. It would be a pity to let that enthusiasm cool down.

The same rules apply to the writing and presentation of the sample material as apply to the writing and presentation of the book as a whole, and these are dealt with more fully in Chapter 7.

*What will happen to your sample material when you have submitted it?*

Again, publishers vary in their practice. It will either be scrutinised in-house by the commissioning editor and whoever else is involved in the decision as to whether or not it should be taken on; or, more likely, it will be scrutinised in-house *and* sent to one or more external reviewers (or 'readers').

A reviewer will typically be an established expert in the field you are writing about and will be asked for an objective assessment of your book on the strength of the proposal and the sample material you have provided. He or she will consider such matters as its accuracy, the soundness of its structure, its suitability to any relevant courses and its general appropriateness to the market at which it is aimed. He or she will normally give an opinion as to whether the book ought to be published, though the final decision will rest with the publisher.

Reviewers are generally very conscientious in their approach and will provide detailed comments on your material. Anonymity is usually preserved, not least to avoid any embarrassment. If the reviewer is a friend or colleague of yours, he or she is unlikely to want to be credited with an uncomplimentary review of your book!

Assuming that the review is generally favourable, the commissioning editor will normally get in touch with you to discuss any important points raised by the reviewer. This may involve another meeting, or may be done by letter or telephone. You may be asked to provide a revised synopsis or sample material taking those points into account, or you may be told that the publishers are happy in principle to take your book on, subject to those points being borne in mind in the writing of it.

In the latter case, you will probably now be sent a copy of the publisher's standard agreement. The time has come to think about terms and timescales.

# Publishers' agreements

Most publishers have printed contracts which form the basis of their agreements with authors. These contracts can generally be amended in certain respects by mutual agreement. Publishers' terms vary, but most contracts will contain clauses covering roughly the same points. These include the basis of the author's remuneration, the timescale for the writing of the book, the nature of the legal relationship between the author and the publisher and various other undertakings by both parties.

Let us look at some of the most common provisions of such agreements:

## Financial terms

As has already been said, all reputable publishers pay their authors. The average non-fiction book may not make your fortune, but you should certainly expect to receive some income from all your hard work.

### *Payment by fee*

Fees tend to be paid mainly to journalists or other professional writers, or for books (such as part-works or popular compendia) where the work is of a very journalistic kind. Under this arrangement, publishers will either agree a fee for writing all or part of a book, payable at various stages from signature of agreement through to publication, or will pay by the number of words.

It is relatively unusual for a publisher to offer a fee for the sort of book we have been discussing. Nor is it necessarily desirable from the author's point of view. A fee removes the risk that you will not make any money if your book fails to sell, but it also removes the possibility of a continuing income if it succeeds.

### *Payment by royalty*

Most authors prefer to take the risk outlined above in the hope of sharing the rewards of continuing success. Most publishers prefer this arrangement too. It is the principle upon which royalty agreements are based and constitutes the most common financial relationship between author and publisher.

A royalty, then, is a percentage of the price of each book sold paid to the author of that book. It may be calculated either on the published price of the book (known as the cover price or list price) or on the price at which the book is actually sold by the publisher (the discounted price or net price), or on a combination of the two. Publishers typically sell books to bookshops at a discount on the cover price of around 30 to 35 per cent. Bookshops then make their money by selling the book to the reader at the cover price. Publishers may sell to book-clubs or to other publishers at higher discounts still.

Royalties vary from about 5 per cent to about 15 per cent. The average is 10 per cent. A quite common arrangement is for publishers to pay 10 per cent of the published price on books sold in the home country and 10 per cent of the net price on books sold overseas. If a book is being produced in both hardback and paperback, it is not uncommon for the royalty to be 10 per cent on the hardback and 7.5 per cent on the paperback, of which more copies would be printed and, one hopes, sold.

Another fairly common arrangement is for the publishers to increase the royalty payable to the author after a certain number of copies of the book have been sold. The threshold for such an increase is sometimes the initial print-run of the book. Thus, a publisher might print 2,500 copies of a book in the first instance and pay the author a 10 per cent royalty on each of these. Once all 2,500 have been sold, the royalty might increase to 12.5 per cent on any reprinted copies. This is sometimes known as an 'escalator'.

Royalties are generally paid yearly or six-monthly. The accounting periods are specified in the contract, and payments are normally made within about three months of the end of those periods. If the royalty income from the book is negligible during any one period, payment may be held over until the end of the next one. The contract will normally specify what the publisher regards as 'negligible'. Some contracts also make provision for a reduced royalty rate below a certain threshold of sales during any one accounting period.

### *Advances against royalties*

It is also quite common for an author to be paid an advance against royalties. An advance is a payment on account and is generally seen by both parties as an act of good faith. Advances are generally paid at one or more of the following stages:

- when the agreement is signed by the author and the publisher
- when an acceptable manuscript is delivered to the publisher by the author
- when the book is published

Except in the case of very well-established authors or famous personalities, advances tend to be modest. They are likely to be a relatively small proportion of the royalties you can expect to receive if the book does well, and will probably not leave you much change after you have paid any secretarial or research costs or set yourself up with a word-processor. Since an advance is a payment on account, you will not receive any royalties on the book until your proportion of the receipts from its sale has exceeded the amount of the advance. Advances are generally non-returnable, unless you fail to deliver or produce a completely unpublishable manuscript.

### Timescale

The contract will specify a date by which the author will deliver the manuscript to the publisher in an acceptable form. This could be anything from six months to two years after the signing of the agreement. In some exceptional cases it could be even longer. The average for a book of around 60,000 words is probably about nine months to a year.

You should always try to agree on a realistic manuscript delivery date and stick to it. Publishers usually publicise their forthcoming books well in advance of publication and delays to schedules can be very disruptive, especially if your book forms part of a series. That said, few publishers include penalty clauses for late delivery in their contracts and most are prepared to be flexible within reasonable limits as long as you keep them fully informed of your progress.

Some publishers include in their standard contracts a commitment to publish within a specified time of receiving an acceptable manuscript unless prevented by circumstances beyond their control (such as printworkers' strikes or acts of God). Chapter 8 gives further details about production timescales (see page 96).

## Copyright and subsidiary rights

### *Copyright*
Under the terms of a typical agreement, the author would retain copyright in the work which forms the subject of that agreement and would licence to the publisher the rights to publish that work in certain territories (usually, in fact, throughout the world). Some publishers prefer the author to make the copyright over to them too. In either case, the term of copyright is established by law and lasts for 50 years after the author's death.

### *Subsidiary rights*
Most publishers also reserve the right to sell certain publishing rights in an author's book to third parties, such as other publishers, book-clubs, magazines, television companies etc. These are known as subsidiary rights and would typically include such uses of your work as the following:

● quotation
● publication in anthologies
● condensation

- reproduction by cassette, gramophone, photography etc.
- electronic and software publishing
- serialisation in newspapers or journals
- sound broadcasting, dramatisation or televisation
- translation

Few of these rights are likely to apply to the average work of non-fiction, but the contract will usually establish a principle for your remuneration if the publisher does succeed in selling any of them. The usual arrangement is for any income from the sale of subsidiary rights to be split between the author and the publisher, often on a 50/50 basis. The same arrangement would normally apply to any royalty income received by the publisher from the sale of the publishing rights in your book to an overseas publisher.

In the case of sales made to book-clubs, it is usual for the author to receive a royalty on the discounted price at which the publisher sells such copies to the book-club rather than for the income to be split in the way described above.

## Other undertakings of author and publisher
In addition to the financial terms, the timescale for delivery and the legal relationship between the author and the publisher, the typical publisher's agreement will also commit the author and the publisher to a number of other undertakings relating to the book.

### *Form of the manuscript*
The publisher's agreement will specify the form in which the manuscript should be delivered to the publisher, which will generally be typed or word-processed in double spacing on A4 paper, and its agreed extent, normally in number of words. It is usual for the publisher to require more than one copy of the manuscript. (There is more about presentation of your material in Chapter 7 – see pages 92 to 95.)

### Proof reading

The contract will also require the author to read the proofs of the work once it has been typeset and to return these proofs to the publisher within a specified period. He or she may also be asked to prepare an index to the work once the final page numbering is known (see page 109).

### Indemnity

The author will be required to indemnify the publisher against action by third parties resulting from the inclusion of any scandalous, libellous, seditious, obscene, plagiarised or otherwise unlawful material in the book. The average work of non-fiction is unlikely to run foul of most of these categories, and the one the publisher will probably be most concerned about is plagiarism. The contract will almost certainly commit you to getting formal permission to include in your book any material drawn from sources of which you do not own the copyright, such as other published books, newspapers and journals, conference material etc. It will also require you to indemnify the publisher against any actions for breach of such copyright. These are standard clauses and you will find few publishers prepared to omit them. (There is more about seeking permissions in Chapter 6 – see page 79.)

### Publishers' control

There will generally be a clause permitting the publishers to edit, produce and market the work in whatever way they think appropriate. Most publishers will want to retain the final say in these matters should any dispute arise, but in practice the editorial process (and to a lesser extent the production and marketing) is generally undertaken in close consultation with the author. (See Chapters 8 and 9 for the details of these processes.) You may also find a clause requiring you to make any amendments to the manuscript that the publishers may request within a specified period after your delivering it to them. This refers to any major changes required before the editorial process can begin.

### Author's costs

Publishers are always very keen to avoid unnecessary changes at proof stage (see page 106), and there will usually be a clause in the contract making you as author liable, above a certain threshold, for the cost of any changes you want to make to the proofs of the book, other than those resulting from typesetters' or publishers' errors. This threshold will probably be expressed as a percentage – often 10 per cent – of the cost of the original typesetting. The purpose of this clause is to avoid authors deciding to rewrite long sections of their book after it has been typeset, since this can be a very expensive process indeed. However, if you know of changes in legislation or other unavoidable developments in the external world which will affect your material between the time you submit the manuscript and the time the book will be published, tell the publishers now. They will almost certainly want to include these and be prepared to bear the resulting cost themselves, but it would be as well to clarify this and, if possible, get something in writing to that effect.

### Complimentary copies

The publishers will undertake to send you a certain number of copies of the book free of charge when it published. Six is a common number. You will also probably find a clause enabling you to buy copies for your own use at a discount comparable to that offered to bookshops by the publishers.

### Reprints and new editions

Most publishers' contracts relate not just to the first printing of the book but to all its future editions too, for as long as the publishers keep it in print. You will therefore find a clause concerning the updating and revision of the book. This will normally commit you to providing revised and updated material for future printings of the book within a reasonable period after the publishers request it. Since the publishers will be making a significant investment by agreeing to publish your book, they will want to be sure that they can continue to publish new editions even if you are unwilling or unable to do so (if you have died, for example). There will therefore usually be a clause enabling the publishers to get someone else to do the work in these circumstances and to pay them out of the royalties you would normally receive.

Some publishers also include a clause under which all rights in the book revert to you if they let the book go out of print and decline to reprint it within a certain period of your requesting them to do so. It is to your advantage to have such a clause in your contract.

### Rival publishers

Finally, there may be a clause preventing you writing a directly competitive book for another publisher. Since it is unlikely that you would want to publish a book which competed head-on with an existing work of yours, this may not worry you. If you have a particular future project in mind, though, and you are not sure whether it might fall within the publishers' definition of a directly competitive work, it might be as well to clarify this now. Apart from anything else, it could be a good way of getting them interested in the book concerned. If they are unsure whether the book is likely to cause a problem – and it will probably be difficult for them to tell at this stage – they may informally ask you to give them first refusal. You may well relish the opportunity to do so.

## Negotiating the contract

The clauses we have been looking at above are not the only ones you can expect to find in a publisher's contract, but they are probably the most common. However, as has already been mentioned, publishers' contracts are often standard agreements which can, within reasonable limits, be amended to reflect the different implications of different books and of the varied circumstances under which they come to be written. It is always worth remembering that, even more than most business contracts, a publisher's agreement is built on a foundation of mutual trust and that a reasonable degree of flexibility can be expected on both sides in its interpretation.

Most negotiations over terms will be conducted in a way that reflects this fact. It is relatively unusual for lawyers to become involved in them, not least because you will probably find your solicitor knows very little about publishing practice and will have little in the way of useful advice to give. If you are a first-time author, it is also unlikely that you will be involving a literary agent in your negotiations (see page 18). So how should you go about discussing the agreement with the publisher?

The golden rule is to query any terms you do not understand or are unhappy about. When you receive a draft contract from the commissioning editor, sit down and go through every clause with a fine tooth comb. Make sure you have understood what everything means. If there is anything you do not understand, or which causes you concern for any reason, make a note of it. If there is anything you would like to include, but which does not appear in the draft agreement, make a note of this too. When you have completed your notes, you should aim to discuss the points one by one with the commissioning editor. If there are a number of points to be dealt with, it might well be best to write a letter in the first instance, in order that you have a clear framework for a later telephone conversation or meeting. If there are only one or two points it might be best to raise them by telephone and then write to confirm the conversation.

A good commissioning editor will be perfectly happy to discuss all these points in whatever detail you feel is necessary. In some cases you may find that an explanation clears up any doubts in your mind. In others, you may find that there is no room for negotiation at all. It is quite likely, though, that the publisher will be prepared to change certain aspects of the wording to accommodate you. Whether this decision can be taken by the commissioning editor on his or her own authority or whether it has to be referred up the publishing hierarchy will depend upon the size and internal structure of the company concerned.

Once you have agreed all the terms of the agreement, you will be sent two copies of a final amended contract for you to sign. These will either be signed and dated by the publishers already or will need to be returned to the publishers for them to sign once you have signed them yourself. You will be sent one copy to keep. It is most important that you keep this copy safely.

You are now a fully signed-up author. The real task of writing your book is about to begin. Before we go on to look at this process in more detail, however, it is worth mentioning two other documents which your publisher will probably send you at this stage.

## The publisher's style sheet and the author's questionnaire

Most publishers have documents which they send to their authors to show how they like their manuscripts to be presented and to ask for various details about the book and the author for marketing purposes. Both of these documents will probably be sent to you with your copy of the signed contract or very soon thereafter.

### The publisher's style sheet

All publishers have what is known as a house style. This means a set of rules relating to spelling, layout and construction of material which is used by the company's editors when they prepare a manuscript for typesetting (see Chapter 8) and is intended to ensure that all the books produced by the company achieve a certain basic consistency in their presentation. These rules are laid out in the company's style sheet.

The style sheet is often a long and detailed document, ranging from rules about spelling (e.g. whether a *z* or an *s* is used in words such as organisation, where either is permissible) to details of how lists should be presented (e.g. with the points shown as 1., 2., 3., or (i), (ii), (iii), or (a), (b), (c), etc.). The more precisely an author's manuscript conforms to these rules when it is delivered to the publisher, the easier will be the copy-editor's task in preparing it for typesetting and printing. Publishers therefore often send authors a copy of their style sheet, or a version of it specially adapted to answer the sort of questions most writers find themselves asking when they first put pen to paper. You should read this document very carefully and should conform to its standards as closely as you possibly can in writing your book. (See Chapter 7, pages 92 to 95, for more about consistency of presentation.)

## The author's questionnaire

Publishers generally begin to market their forthcoming books well in advance of publication, and often well in advance of receiving a completed manuscript. To do this without misleading potential purchasers, they have to be sure they have full and accurate information about the form a book will take, and no-one is in a better position to provide that information than the author of the book concerned.

Either when you sign the contract or at a later stage, you will therefore probably be sent a questionnaire to fill in, giving such details as:

- your name, address and telephone number

- your biographical details

- the likely title of your book

- other books on the subject and how yours will distinguish itself from them

- the readership you are aiming at and how your approach will be tailored to it

- any courses your book will be relevant to

- any specific points you feel should be brought out in the marketing

- any specific individuals, journals, magazines, newspapers etc. whom you feel should be made aware of the book and/or sent copies to review on publication

You should aim to fill in this questionnaire as fully and as promptly as you can. (If you have produced the sort of detailed proposal discussed in Chapter 4, you will already have most of the material you need for the purpose.) It is worth taking time and care over it, since for many publishers the author's questionnaire will form the springboard for the entire marketing campaign. Not only catalogue entries, but also advance information for bookshops and members of the sales force will be based on it. At a later stage, the 'blurb' which appears on the back cover or inside flap of the book will probably draw heavily on it too.

# 6

# Researching your Book

You have signed your contract and agreed with the publisher that you will deliver a finished manuscript by a particular date, which at the moment probably seems a very long way off. After asking yourself as honestly as possible whether you are really able to write the proposed book, you have convinced yourself that you can and have been able to convince a publisher of the same. Now it is time to put that conviction into practice.

The research process is a crucial part of the work of writing any non-fictional book. If your book is about a subject you have been interested in for many years, you will probably already know some parts of it very well indeed. However, there will probably be other parts you do not know quite so well and still others you know hardly at all. When you were pursuing your subject for interest, there was no need to develop a detailed understanding of those parts of it which interested you least or were most difficult to find out about. But now that you are committed to writing a book about it, the situation is very different. You must ensure that you know enough about every part of your subject to be able to inform the reader as fully about it as the structure and level of your book demand.

The *Concise Oxford Dictionary* defines research as 'careful search or inquiry...; endeavour to discover new or collate old facts etc. by scientific study of a subject, course of critical investigation'. This definition tends to imply that research is a process undertaken mainly for its own sake, or at least to acquire knowledge for its own sake. Much research is certainly of this kind. It is 'pure' research. But the kind of research you will need to do in order to write your book is not. It is basically 'applied' research. You are not setting out to know everything there is to know about your field, and you do not necessarily have to 'discover new ... facts' about it. You *do* have to know enough to be able to write an accurate and informative book for your target reader in the time available.

So how should you go about organising your research?

## Sources of help and information

There are three main categories of information source for the researcher of a work of non-fiction, all of which may be useful in differing degrees according to the type of book you are writing and the type of reader it is aimed at. They are:

- published sources

- unpublished sources

- personal experience

Let us look briefly at what each of these categories includes.

### Published sources

#### *Books, journals and magazines*
As has already been said, it is essential to know what competitive books there are on your subject when you are researching the market for your book. If you have followed the approach suggested in Chapters 2 and 3, you will already have identified the main books in your field. You may own a number of them and will have seen a number of others at the library. These will be equally essential to you when you come to research the book itself.

Books are obviously a major resource for the researcher on any subject. But they are not always the best place to go for information. For example, they may be pitched at the wrong level to provide the kind of information you want for your own book, or they may be out of date, especially in fast-changing fields. In most specialist or semi-specialist subject areas, then, you will need to supplement the information you derive from books with more frequently published or precisely targeted information sources, such as specialist journals and magazines, some of which you may already subscribe to. The specialist pages of more general magazines and newspapers can also be helpful sources of up-to-the-minute information. (Many libraries store journals and newspapers on microfiche.) In all these types of media, however, it is as well to remember that the very tight deadlines journalists have to work to do not always provide the best conditions for reliability.

### Reports and surveys
In addition to books, journals and magazines, a number of organisations – from companies to trade associations – publish specialist reports or surveys in their particular areas of interest.

### Database information
In recent years there has been an explosion of electronically stored information, much of which can be accessed on-line by members of the public. In specialist fields where the pace of change is very rapid, such on-line databases are likely to be the most reliable and up-to-date sources of information. However, they can be expensive to access and you will need to be very sure of your requirements to avoid running up costly search fees.

### Libraries
Before leaving the question of published sources of information, it is worth saying a few more words about libraries. It is easy to overlook the treasure-house of information and advice which a good library represents. Think of your library not just as a place to go for specific details, but also as a means of discovering alternative sources of information.

Time spent familiarising yourself with the library's catalogues is always time well spent. Most libraries will have a catalogue of their holdings by subject as well as by author. They will also either keep or have access to an array of important bibliographical aids, such as *British Books in Print* (which, as the title suggests, lists all books in print in Great Britain). Most too will operate an inter-library loan system, which means that they can normally get hold of a copy of a book even if they don't stock it themselves.

While public libraries vary a great deal in the amount of material they keep, there are nowadays many more specialist libraries than there used to be. Some of these may be attached to colleges, companies or government departments, but are nonetheless open to members of the public. It is always worth inquiring about the conditions under which such libraries can be used.

Remember too that librarians themselves can be an invaluable source of help and advice. They are information experts who are particularly skilled at identifying the best sources to go to in order to find information on a particular subject. They may not be able to tell you which book is the best one to read on, say, the Brazilian coffee crop, but they will generally be able to refer you to other published sources which can. They may also be able to advise on libraries with specialist holdings.

**Unpublished sources**
In addition to the sort of published information mentioned above, there are also a number of unpublished sources which you may well find it useful to draw on in researching your book. These include not only unpublished documents such as letters, lecture notes or in-company training material, but also the findings of original research by interviews.

For certain types of non-fiction writing, such sources can be very important. The more practical the book, the more likely it is that its usefulness to the reader will be enhanced by the inclusion of case study material or worked examples relating to people's real-life experience. For example, if you were writing a book on careers in agriculture aimed at the school-leaver, he or she would no doubt find it almost as illuminating to read what another recent school-leaver has to say about his or her experience of working on a farm as to be given pages of objective description. Similarly, if you were writing a book on investing in the stock market, a few worked examples of how real portfolios performed might be worth pages of technical explanation about price-earnings ratios and yield curves.

You may be able to supply some of these sorts of example from your own personal experience (see page 78 below). But no-one can be sure of how typical their own experience is until they test it against other people's. If yours is the sort of book which might benefit from the inclusion of real-life examples, there is no substitute for actually going out and speaking to people who have first-hand experience of the kind of things you want to write about.

It is worth bearing in mind, though, that people can be nervous of appearing in print and that you may therefore have to establish your bona fides very clearly in your initial letter or telephone conversation. That said, if people are confident that your book is to be produced by a reputable publisher and will serve a genuinely useful purpose for others who are interested in their field of activity, most will be quite willing to share their experiences with you. Always make sure, though, that you know whether they wish to be identified in the book. Some people may be prepared to speak more freely if what they say will appear only as an anonymous example. Check, too, whether they would like to see what you intend to write about them before you submit it to the publisher. While this can slow things up, it is a proper courtesy and will also help avoid future complaints of misinterpretation. Remember that you may need to approach the same people again when you come to write future editions of your book (see page 120).

Personal interviews can also be supplemented by postal or telephone interviews. But whether you are contacting someone face-to-face, over the telephone or by letter, you will need to have a very clear idea of what you want to elicit from them before you begin. In the case of a postal approach, this can be formalised by means of a questionnaire. In the case of a personal or telephone interview, it is best to have a written list of questions to use as a basis for discussion. Only ask what is relevant to the material you want to write and make sure that you have all the information you need on each of these points. If you want to compare different people's experiences in the book, remember that you will need to have the same basic information about everyone involved.

Above all, bear the information needs of your readers firmly in mind when drawing up your questions and conducting the interview itself. It is only too easy to forget that you are effectively interviewing on their behalf. You are therefore mainly concerned not with what *you* want to know but with what *they* will want to know when they read your book.

### Personal experience

Perhaps the most important source of information you have available to you is your own fund of personal experience. Unfortunately, it is also the hardest to access objectively.

Not only is it difficult, as mentioned above, to be sure that your own experience is typical until you have tested it against other people's; it is also very difficult to step far enough back from a subject in which you have a deep personal involvement to be able to see what a reader, perhaps coming to it for the first time, will need to know about it. Many authors say that achieving this distance is one of the hardest tasks in writing a work of non-fiction.

For all the problems it presents, though, there is no doubt that personal experience lends conviction to any writing. From the moment you begin to develop the idea for your book, it is worth regarding what happens to you on a daily basis as a potential source of material and making notes on it accordingly. Today's disaster may be tomorrow's cautionary tale!

# Originality and plagiarism

## Defining originality

Research inevitably raises the question of originality. It will be clear from what has already been said in this chapter that, whatever the subject of your book, you are bound to have to draw on other people's published work in the writing of it. However, as we have seen, most publishers' contracts include a clause whereby the author guarantees that the book he or she is writing is an 'original work' and does not breach any existing copyright. How can you reconcile these two requirements? Where does debt to others' knowledge end and plagiarism begin? These are difficult questions, and such rules as there are are not always easy to interpret. However, there are certain basic guidelines.

## Copyright law

First of all, it is important to realise that there is no copyright in ideas. There is, however, copyright in the *form* in which ideas are expressed, whether verbally or pictorially.

Works remain in copyright for 50 years after the death of their author, or for 50 years after publication if they are first published after the author's death. If you want to quote from a work which falls outside these limits, you can generally do so without seeking permission from anybody. However, if you want to quote at any length from a work which is still in copyright, or want to use an illustration from it, you must seek the permission of the copyright holder to do so. (In practice, it may not always be necessary to seek formal permission for short quotations, but since interpretations of 'short' can vary a great deal, the golden rule is 'better safe than sorry'.)

## Seeking copyright permission

In most cases this will mean writing to the publisher of the work in which the passage or illustration you want to use appears, even if the copyright is the author's. Some publishers will make standard charges for the use of material, depending upon the length of the quotation and the territories in which your book will be sold. You will generally have to pay these charges yourself. Others will simply want you to include an acknowledgement of the source of the material in your book and may specify the form of words to be used. Remember: it is not sufficient to acknowledge the source of a quotation without seeking the formal permission of the copyright holder.

It is important to remember that there is copyright in unpublished work too. An author's words are protected by copyright from the minute he/she puts pen to paper. If you want to quote from a typed hand-out given by the speaker to all the delegates at a conference you attended, or if you want to use material from an in-house training manual put together by one of your staff, you will have to seek their permission to do so.

If for any reason you are unsure whether a work from which you wish to quote is still in copyright, it is always best to apply the 'better safe than sorry' rule. Actions for breach of copyright can be long and expensive and will be very bad for your reputation as an author, not least with your own publisher.

### *Plagiarism*
The more difficult area, of course, is that of 'ideas'. Here the guidelines are somewhat hazier. Most works of non-fiction which are published can be said to add to the sum total, if not of knowledge, then at least of understanding, of their field. When is it plagiarism to draw on that body of information?

It is impossible to give a precise answer that will be equally valid in all cases. Perhaps the best advice is simply to observe the basic rules of courtesy and common sense. If you are quoting passages from somebody else's work with only cosmetic changes, then you can reasonably expect trouble from that somebody else if he or she finds out about it. Again, if you are drawing almost exclusively on a single source for all or part of your work – if a whole chapter or a whole section of a chapter, say, are virtually paraphrases of somebody else's book – then you are likely to run into problems with the original author. These sorts of unattributed borrowings are unacceptable. If you know your subject as thoroughly as you should to have got this far, they will also be unnecessary.

If, on the other hand, you are working from a number of different sources, thoroughly assimilating what they say to the structure and requirements of your own book and using them as a means of substantiating your own arguments, then you will not generally be courting any difficulties. This is a perfectly legitimate process. If it were not, the whole idea of research from existing material would become meaningless.

Between these two poles, of course, there are a number of grey areas. What do you do, for example, if you are writing a book on the care of young children and wish to describe a particular type of toilet training which was recommended in a published book and which you have found to be especially effective? Or if you are indebted to a particular legal textbook for the legal section of an otherwise general book? If you are not sure about any particular case, your publisher may be able to advise you. If you are still unsure, apply the 'better safe than sorry' rule and write to the publishers of the other book, explaining the situation and outlining what you intend to say.

## Working methods

Authors work in many different ways, depending upon their temperament and the type of book they are writing. What best suits any individual is bound to be largely a matter of taste and practice. However, the suggestions which follow are likely to be applicable whatever the book you are researching.

### Making a start

Start your research the minute the idea for the book occurs to you. While the most intensive period of research is bound to come only when you have signed your contract, there is much you can do before then.  As we have seen, a great deal of the research you will have to do in order to put together a persuasive proposal for potential publishers will also be very useful when you come to start work on the book itself.  This research will bring you into close contact with what else has been written on your subject just when the idea is freshest in your mind.  Do not let the ideas you come across at this stage slip through your net simply because they are not of immediate use.  Start making notes now.  They will be very useful later – both when you have to decide whether you can really draw on enough material to be able to write the book and when, having persuaded yourself and your publisher that you can, you start the actual writing.

### Making notes

Always make very full notes on anything you think may prove useful.  It is very easy, as you are swept along by the argument of a particular book or a journal article, to believe that you will never forget its finer points.  You will.  The next day you will read something equally compelling, and the day after that something more enthralling still.  You dare not trust your memory to summon up all the points of all these passages at will, whenever the need arises.  Nor can you guarantee that brief two- or three-word notes will be a sufficient trigger months after the event.  Whenever you are making notes on any research material, imagine yourself looking back on them in the future and make sure they answer the questions you will be asking *then*.

It often helps to achieve this objective if you make your notes not as you read each sentence, but after you have finished reading a particular passage (and preferably without permitting yourself to refer back to the text as you do so).  Most of us read with greater concentration if we know we have to summarise what we have read afterwards – if only for ourselves – than if we jot down points of detail as we go along without relating them to the overall structure of what we are reading.

When researching a work of non-fiction it is essential to make a note of all your sources. If the source is a book, these notes should include the name of the author, the title, the publishers, the date of publication and the relevant page numbers. If it is a journal article, it should include the name and date of issue of the journal, the publishers, the page number and the journalist's name where appropriate. You will need all these details for your bibliography or footnotes (if you are using them – see page 93). They will also reduce the risk of your accidentally passing off other authors' material as your own. Remember that you may not look at any given page of notes for many months after they were originally written. Can you guarantee that you can distinguish your own thoughts from other people's after all that time?

## Making order out of chaos

During the course of your research you will accumulate quantities of paper: sheets of handwritten notes, pieces of typescript, photocopies, newspaper cuttings. Precisely how you choose to organise this material will depend to some extent on the type of book you are writing. The essential requirement, though, is that you should be able to refer back to information as quickly and reliably as possible.

From a purely practical point of view, it is worth ensuring that all your papers are as far as possible the same size – A4 being the best standard. This will mean photocopying such oddments as cuttings or pasting them down onto A4 sheets. When doing so, always ensure that the date and source of the cutting are marked.

It is also essential to file all your papers by subject. At as early a stage of the process as possible you should try to marry those subjects up with the structure of your book. When you have finalised your synopsis, you could do worse than buy a series of folders or box files and write one chapter title on each. As your research progresses you might then sub-divide each file by the main headings of the chapter concerned. This method will ensure that everything likely to be of use in a particular section of the book is filed in a single easily accessible place.

## Calling a halt

There is never likely to come a time when you feel you have done all the research you need to do. In practice you will probably find that the research and the writing of your book soon start to overlap one another. You will probably find yourself starting to write one chapter while still researching others. But it is perhaps worth ending this chapter with the advice with which we began it. Remember that you do not need to know everything there is to know about your subject before you start to write your book, even if it were possible to do so. You do need, though, to know as much as is required to give an accurate and informative account of that subject to the sort of reader your book is aimed at.

The temptation to do more and more research is a strong one. Within limits it is a healthy one too. But you will know you have reached those limits when you find yourself using the research as an excuse to put off starting the writing. There can be few authors who do not find themselves reaching this point at some stage in the gestation of a book. It is definitely the point at which to put pen to paper!

And that is the subject of the next chapter.

# 7

# Writing your Book

The weeks of preparation are over. You have shaped your idea into the outline of a book and persuaded a publisher that it is saleable. You have done, or are in the process of doing, your initial research. The time has come to start on the real work of writing.

From where you now stand, the task will probably look very much more daunting than it did when you originally put together your proposal. However rigorously you considered your ideas at that stage, you will find you have new problems to solve and new challenges to meet as you begin to put flesh on the bones of your synopsis. The process of writing throws up unforeseen difficulties at every turn.

This chapter looks at some of the basic principles of writing non-fiction in an attempt to help minimise some of those difficulties. But it can only hope to scratch the surface of a subject on which complete books have been written in their own right. As has already been said, writers work in many different ways and you will only discover the ways which suit you best by trial and error. If you are lucky, you will make the discovery in time for it to help you with your first book. If not, it will certainly help you with your next one!

# Getting the structure right

The most immediate problem you will be faced with is that of imposing a structure on something that does not yet exist. The synopsis you drew up for the publisher will already have gone a long way towards defining this structure. But you will need to define it more exactly still as you start to write. How should you do this?

## Thinking in terms of units

It is an enormous help to think of the book as a series of individual units rather than as a single seamless whole. In the light of your research, you can review your original synopsis to ensure that the balance of the constituent parts is still correct. Once you are confident that it is, you can concentrate on the parts in turn, planning and writing each unit individually. It is very much easier to think of writing a complete section of, say, 1,000 words over the next two days, than to think of writing 60,000 words over the next two or three months.

The main units will obviously be the individual chapters as outlined in your synopsis. For the purposes of organising the actual writing, though, it is best to think of the text under each main heading, or even under each subheading, as a separate unit. Your first task is to define the length of each of these units. How should you do this?

## Defining the length of each unit

Begin with the total word target specified in your contract. When this was drawn up, of course, neither you nor the commissioning editor could have been sure of the ideal length for your book. The number of words you have committed yourself to delivering will therefore probably have been estimated on the basis of broadly similar books on the publisher's list. However, while it is necessarily a guideline rather than a firm limit, you should aim to meet this word target as closely as you can. Slight undershooting or overshooting will not be disastrous, but a major deviation from the contractual stipulation may well be. Most publishers draw up budgets and marketing plans for their books well in advance of publication, and the length of a book can materially affect both the cost of producing it and its saleability to the target readership. A book contracted to contain 60,000 words is unlikely to be unpublishable if the final manuscript runs to 65,000 words. It may be if it runs to 100,000.

Your contractual target, then, is a very useful starting-point for determining the length of the individual units. We saw in Chapter 4 how you could build up to an estimated total length by estimating the length of the individual parts in relation to each other (see page 47). Now you can effectively reverse this process and estimate the length of the individual sections by breaking them down from the total.

In so doing, start from the (artificial) assumption that the chapters will be of roughly equal length. Then – since not all the chapters will in fact be of equal importance – adjust the planned length of each according to its significance in the overall scheme. Repeat the process for each subsection of each chapter and note the resulting individual word targets against the headings which represent each of those subsections in your synopsis. You are bound to miss most of these targets to a greater or lesser extent as you write the text itself. But it is far better to adjust them as you go than to start without them.

## Planning the content of each unit

Your next job is to plan the content of each section in more detail. You will already have given a fair amount of thought to this, both in drawing up your original synopsis and, to an even greater extent, in estimating the length of each subsection. Now is the time to formalise those thoughts.

On the whole, you will find that the tighter the brief you give yourself, the easier you will find it to write and the better the resulting material will be. That said, ideas necessarily evolve in the process of writing. You will almost certainly find yourself taking unexpected detours on the way to your destination as new possibilities occur to you. This kind of unpredictability is one of the most exciting aspects of the experience of writing. But it must be unpredictability within a solid overall framework. Detours can reveal important features along the way; but unless you have a map of your route they will soon become directionless wanderings.

Whether you fill in all the details of that route now, or whether you plan out only the immediate lie of the land ahead, is very much a matter for the individual writer. But you should certainly know in detail what you are going to say in each unit before you start writing it. In practice, this will mean noting all the salient points you intend to cover in the section concerned and having an idea of how much text you want to devote to each. If you think of each main point as a paragraph, you should aim to know what each paragraph will cover before you begin to write the section.

The process of drafting out this detailed structure is likely to be very similar to that described for drafting a synopsis in Chapter 4 (see page 50). In the first instance, note down your thoughts for the particular section randomly as they occur to you. You can begin to sort them into a logical order later, as patterns begin to emerge from your initial jottings.

### Planning your schedule

As we mentioned at the beginning of the last chapter, your contractual date for delivering a completed manuscript will probably seem a very long way off when you sign your agreement. Do not be fooled. It will creep up on you very fast.

Perhaps the most important thing is not to yield to the temptation to relax once you have finalised your contract. Now is the time to capitalise on the enthusiasm you have worked up during the drafting of your proposal. Plan out your time in as much detail as you can from the first day. Set aside so much time for research and so much time for writing each section of the book. Build in time at the end of the process to review and revise the material and, if necessary, to have parts or all of it looked over by other people. If you can allow enough time to be able to put the complete draft of the manuscript aside for a week or so before giving it a final (and ideally more objective) read through, it is well worth doing so.

If, despite all your best efforts, you find yourself running behind schedule, it is essential to give your commissioning editor good warning of the likely delay, so that the publishing schedules can be adjusted accordingly. If there is bad news to be told, he/she would much rather be told it in time to make contingency plans than receive a sheepish phonecall a week before the manuscript is due to be delivered.


# Getting the words onto paper

At the end of the last chapter we spoke of putting pen to paper. This is increasingly becoming a misnomer. As has already been said, when publishers say manuscript, they *always* mean typescript or word-processed material. No publisher today will accept a handwritten manuscript.

How you arrive at your typescript, of course, is very much a matter of personal preference. Some writers prefer to write their first draft in longhand and then revise as they type. Some dictate and have their tapes professionally typed up. Others work directly on the typewriter. But nowadays more and more writers are working directly on to computers or word-processors.

### Word-processing

If you are about to embark on a full-length book and do not have word-processing facilities, it would be very well worth looking into the possibility of acquiring them. The price of equipment has plummeted over the last 10 years or so and is now well within the reach of the average pocket. Most systems are also easy to get to grips with, and the convenience of being able to revise your copy freely, quickly and simply before printing it out is worth a couple of weeks of intensive self-tuition. You may even be able to persuade your publishers to cover the cost of your investment with an advance against royalties, especially if they foresee savings in the time and cost of production from being able to use your disks for typesetting purposes.

We shall have more to say about the physical and stylistic presentation of your manuscript later in this chapter (see pages 92 to 95 below). First of all, though, it is worth considering one or two basic principles of successful book-writing.

### Remember who you are writing for

This has been said more than once during the course of this book, but it is never more important than now when you are actually doing the writing. Test every sentence of every paragraph of every chapter against the requirements of the target reader you identified in your proposal. Are you giving him/her the right information at the right time and in the right way? Asking yourself these questions will soon cease to be a conscious process and will become second nature. But even when you think it has, it is worth trying to catch yourself out occasionally!

### Don't feel you have to write the book in chapter order

It is rare for authors of non-fiction to start with the first chapter and work doggedly through to the last one (just as it is rare for readers of non-fiction to do so). The Introduction, for example, almost always gets written last of all. You will be sure to know the subjects of some sections better than others and it is generally best to start on these, even if they occur halfway through the book.

The danger of this approach, of course, is that omissions or overlaps between chapters are more easily overlooked. For example, there is always a temptation to explain things fully the first time you mention them. But if you are writing the later chapters first, your first encounter with a particular term or subject may not coincide with your reader's. Cross-referencing thoroughly as you go – even if this means cross-referring to things you have not yet written – will help alert you to such potential oversights when you read through your manuscript in order for the first time.

### Follow the structure, not the research

It is also important to govern what you have to say by the structure you have laid down and not by the research you have done. You will have discovered during your research that you cannot draw neat lines around subjects. Apparently separate subjects intersect at many points and it is easy to be tempted into irrelevance by trying to include in your book as much of what you have found out in your research as you possibly can. Resist the temptation. If you don't, it will be only too obvious to the reader when and why you have given in to it. Again, test everything against your detailed plan – and therefore against the information needs of your target reader. Digress only where he/she will find it useful.

### The curse of every author – writer's block

There will certainly be days when you sit in front of a blank sheet of paper for hours on end without finding the words to put down on it. You will believe you have dried up for good. You will wonder why you ever thought you could write a book.

The only answer is to write *something*. If the section you are working on won't flow, stop working on it and start on another one. If that one won't flow either, try a third. If you don't seem able to get anything to work, pick out some of the technical terms you will be using in the book and start to define them. If you won't be using many technical terms, take some of the less technical ones and look them up in the dictionary. If their dictionary definitions don't seem to fit the senses in which you want to use them, write your own. This often helps to overcome the initial block. If all else fails, turn to one of the competitive books and read a few pages. There is nothing like disagreeing with what somebody else has to say about your subject to get the creative wheels turning!

Above all, don't just sit back and wait for inspiration to strike you. Without provocation, it won't.

# Style and presentation

This is not a treatise on the use of the English language. There are plenty of excellent books already available on the art of communication. But no book on how to get published would be complete without considering what publishers look for in the style and presentation of a manuscript.

## *House style*

As has already been mentioned, most publishers have a 'house style' and produce style sheets embodying its main rules. Many also produce versions of this style sheet specially designed for their authors. If you have not been sent a document of this kind, ask for one. If you have, read it very carefully and follow its precepts as closely as possible in preparing your manuscript. Details will naturally vary between different publishing houses, but the ultimate aim of all is to ensure the maximum degree of clarity and consistency. If, after reading the style sheet and any other guidance notes the publisher may issue, you still have queries about presentational matters, always contact your commissioning editor to resolve them. It is worth ironing out any wrinkles at an early stage. If you don't, the copy-editor will only have to do so later (see pages 100 to 105).

## *Headings*

It is crucial to maintain a consistent system of headings, since these will be vital signposts to the reader as he/she explores the new territory of your book. The importance of establishing a logical hierarchy of headings and sticking to it has already been mentioned in Chapter 4 (see page 51). But it is essential to check at every stage of the writing that all the material included under any particular heading really belongs there and that the heading itself belongs under any higher level of heading which may precede it.

In the printed book, the different levels of heading will be distinguished by different typestyles. When preparing your manuscript, though, the main requirement is to indicate the ranking of each heading in the hierarchy. The conventional means of indicating this ranking is by designating the different levels of heading A, B, C, etc., where A is either a chapter heading or a main heading within a chapter.

## Illustrations

Similarly, it is important to be clear and consistent in your choice and use of any illustrations. Most publishers prefer these to be separated out from the manuscript, individually captioned and given figure numbers, each being keyed into the text in the position where it would be best for it to appear. The typesetter or printer will ensure that the finished illustration appears as close to this position as possible. All figures should be referred to in the text.

## Bibliographies and footnotes

The publishers' style sheet will also specify conventions for such things as bibliographical references and footnotes. (For example, for non-academic works most publishers prefer to avoid footnotes altogether, or at least to place them at the end of each chapter or at the end of the book rather than at the foot of the page to which they refer, the latter being both more expensive to typeset and generally more distracting for the reader.)

## Prelims

When the publishers edit the book they will make up the preliminary material which will precede the main text in the published version (these pages are known as 'prelims' and include the title page, the copyright page, etc.). There is no need for you to provide the copy for all of these yourself. It is helpful, though, if you can draw up a contents list, giving at least all the chapter headings and main headings within chapters. Since you will not know the final page numbers at this stage, you can either add the numbers of the manuscript sheets (which are known as 'folios' until they are typeset) or give no numbers at all. Similarly, if you want to include cross-references in the text, type 'see page 000' and mark the folio number in the margin in pencil. This will help you to identify the references when you come to read the final page proofs (see page 106). The index which will appear at the back of the book is also normally produced at the page proof stage (see page 109).

### The presentation of the manuscript

It is not just the substance of your manuscript that should conform to the basic rules of clarity and consistency. Its physical appearance should too. You should always deliver the top copy of your manuscript and ensure that the material is typed on one side of the paper only, using the same typeface throughout. Everything should be double-spaced, including passages of quotation, lists, captions, etc.). This is because, as we shall see in Chapter 8, the manuscript will have to be edited and marked up by the publisher and there must be room for him/her to do so without it becoming incomprehensible to the typesetters and printers. For the same reason you should leave adequate margins – say, 30-50 mm – on the right- and particularly the left-hand side of the page as well as reasonable spaces at the top and bottom of each sheet. Always use the same size of paper throughout, plain white A4 (297 x 210 mm) or the slightly smaller size represented by most continuous computer stationery, being virtually standard. Keep any handwritten amendments to an absolute minimum.

There is no need to spiral-bind your manuscript or to deliver it in a ring-binder. Do not staple, tag or paperclip the pages together. While you may think this makes things easier for the publisher, it does not. The editor will want to read loose sheets and will only have to separate them if you have bound them together in any way. (If you are using continuous stationery, separate the sheets yourself.) It is best to number the folios consecutively throughout the manuscript and not just consecutively within chapters. This can be done in pencil at the top of each sheet. If you need to interpolate any lengthy passages after the bulk of the text has been typed and numbered, type them on a separate sheet and number it

'– A', where – is the number of the sheet on which the interpolated passage should appear. Indicate where the passage should be inserted by some such words as 'Take in copy from p – A attached'.

### Making sure the manuscript is complete

Finally, remember that the manuscript you send to the publisher should be, as far as you are concerned, the final version of the book. If there are parts still to be written, write them before you send it; the publishers will normally want a complete manuscript and will not be able to start work on it until they have one. If there are passages you are not happy with, change them now. If you want to send parts of it to friends or colleagues for their comments, do so at this stage and incorporate their suggestions before you deliver it.

Then, once you are sure you have done all you can, allow yourself a few moments of self-satisfaction before despatching your *magnum opus* on the next stage of its journey into print!

# 8

# What Happens to your Manuscript?

You have put the final full stop to the final sentence of your manuscript. You have tested your patience and your powers of endurance – not to mention those of your friends and family – to the very limit. You have written your book. What happens now?

You might be forgiven for wanting to put your feet up and forget all about the subject you have been living with so intimately for so long. Unfortunately, you will have to delay that luxury for a little longer. The most intensive period of your work on the book is over, but the publishers' is just beginning. And you play as essential a part in what remains to be done before the book can be published as the editors, the typesetters or the printers.

It can take publishers anything from three months to a year or more to produce a book from the day when your manuscript falls on the desk of the commissioning editor who signed you up. The average production time is probably about six to nine months from receipt of an acceptable manuscript to publication. For most of this time you will have an important role to play and will be in regular contact with various members of the publishing company's staff. It is therefore important to know the stages of the road your manuscript still has to travel before it becomes the book you will now be eagerly looking forward to seeing.

# From manuscript to published book

The process by which an author's manuscript becomes a published book comprises a number of consecutive stages. Precisely what each stage involves and what part the author plays in it will vary between publishers, but the following is a typical progression:

- the manuscript is read by the commissioning editor and/or out-of-house readers

- the author is asked to make any major alterations as necessary

- the manuscript, amended as necessary, is passed to the copy-editor who edits for consistency, house style etc.

- any queries raised by the copy-editorial process are resolved with the author

- the edited manuscript is sent to the typesetter who produces typeset proofs

- the proofs are sent to the author to be read and corrected as necessary; at the same time they are read by the copy-editor

- the corrected proofs are sent back to the typesetters for the corrections to be typeset; the typesetter sends revised proofs to the publisher

- when the typesetting is finalised it is sent to the printers for the book's pages and jacket to be printed

- when the printing is finished the printed sheets and jackets are sent to the binders to be bound up as finished books, which are then delivered to the publisher's warehouse

As we saw in Chapter 1, very few publishers have the facilities to perform every stage of this process themselves. The vast majority are heavily reliant on the services of out-of-house suppliers – from freelance editors to typesetters, printers and binders – throughout the production of a book. They are also very reliant on your involvement as the book's author right up to the point where the finished typesetting (generally known as 'camera-ready copy' – see page 113) is sent to the printers.

Now let us look at each of these stages in greater detail.

## Submitting your manuscript

Before sending your manuscript, check your contract to make sure you are sending everything the publisher requires. For example, many contracts ask for two copies of the finished manuscript, so that the publisher can send one to an outside reader or to potential co-publishers.

If you are sending your material through the post, ensure that you do so in a form which can be traced it if it goes astray. Ask at the Post Office to find out which method of delivery they recommend. Keep any receipts you are given and make a note of the date the manuscript was sent. If you are sending two copies, it is worth the expense of sending them in separate packages. Above all, *keep a copy of the manuscript*. It is also as well to forewarn the commissioning editor by telephone that the manuscript is about to be put in the post so that he or she can watch out for it and alert you if it fails to arrive when it should do. Ask the publishers to acknowledge safe receipt of the material and if you hear nothing from them within a few days of your committing the package to the post, ring up to check whether it has arrived.

You may prefer to deliver the manuscript by hand, unless of course you live in Cornwall and your publisher is based in Inverness. There is considerable comfort in knowing that you have placed the child of all your labours in the hands of your publisher in person. But do remember that commissioning editors cannot read 60,000 words in five minutes and do not expect an instant intelligent reaction to what you have written!

## Publishers' readers

The first thing that will happen is that the commissioning editor will read your manuscript and/or send it to an outside reader. What will they be looking for?

### The initial review
The main purpose of reading your manuscript at this stage is to

ensure that it conforms to the brief you originally agreed with the commissioning editor and to check that there are no obvious structural or technical shortcomings in the material. Except in the most technical subjects, most publishers will feel confident of being able to judge the *structural* soundness of the material they are sent. Except in the least technical subjects, however, or where the author is indisputably the leading authority in his or her field, most will not feel confident of judging the *technical* soundness of that material. They will therefore send it to one or more readers to ask for a detailed critical review.

These readers will be experts in your subject. They may even be the same people who reviewed your sample material at the outset. But now they will not be asked whether or not your book is publishable, but what in their view needs to be improved, corrected or reviewed to make it as appropriate to its target market as possible. If, for example, the book is geared to a particular academic syllabus, they will be expected to point out any areas where, in their opinion, your treatment is pitched too high or too low for students of that syllabus. They will also point out any errors of fact.

Meanwhile, your commissioning editor will probably be reading the book with much the same considerations in mind, although in his or her case it will be the structural aspects of the book and their appropriateness to the market that will be of the greatest concern. For example, have you achieved a proper balance between the various parts of the book or have you given undue weight to some at the expense of others? Have you suddenly changed your system of headings halfway through? Have you quoted statistics that will clearly be out of date by the time the book is published? Do you refer only to the U.K. where you should be referring to all English-speaking countries?

Neither the commissioning editor nor the reader will be concerned with such minutiae as spelling and typing errors, but both may note down any minor structural points which need not be referred to you but which will need to be ironed out during the copy-editing. When the commissioning editor receives the reader's report, he/she will collate it with any points he/she feels should be addressed before the manuscript can be passed to the copy-editor for the more detailed editing, and will raise all these points with you.

### *Amending the text*

It is very rare for a manuscript to be thought so poor as to be unsalvageable at this stage, and the most likely outcome of this initial review procedure is that you will be asked your opinion on any contentious issues and requested to make a few relatively minor amendments. Even in the rare event of your manuscript being found to need major surgery, the commissioning editor will probably ask to meet you to discuss the details of what is required and to set a timescale for any rewriting, rather than tell you that your book is unpublishable. After all, the publishers will have been sufficiently confident of the market for it for them to have taken you on as an author and paid you an advance against royalties. They will have approved the synopsis to which you will have been writing. And they will probably have begun to market your book already. (That said, the case may be very different if you have completely ignored your original synopsis or written a book aimed at schoolchildren when you were signed up to write one for university students.)

If very little needs amending, the commissioning editor may pass a list of minor suggestions to the copy-editor with the manuscript and ask him or her to collate these with any queries that may arise from the copy-editorial work. Whether this is the case, or whether you have been asked to make certain amendments yourself, when the manuscript is finished to the commissioning editor's satisfaction, the next stage will be the copy-editing.

## Copy-editing

Copy-editing is the process of preparing a manuscript for the printer. It is very rare for this to be done by the same person who commissioned the book, although this may be the case in smaller publishing houses. Generally, though, the copy-editor (who may also be known as a desk editor, a house editor, a sub-editor or just an editor) will be part of a separate branch of the editorial department from the commissioning editor. He/she may report either to the commissioning editor who has overall responsibility for your book or to a managing editor who has overall responsibility for ensuring that the editing of all the publisher's books goes smoothly and to schedule.

Increasingly publishers are using the services of freelance editors, whose work is co-ordinated by the editorial department in-house. Under such an arrangement you may deal with an in-house editor who effectively acts as an executive middleman between you as author and the freelance editor who is actually copy-editing your book. Whether the actual editing is done in-house or by a freelance, you have a right to expect that the in-house editor will be fully conversant with your manuscript, as will indeed normally be the case.

Many authors think of editing – if they think of editing at all – as a rather cosmetic, mechanical procedure. It is not. A good editor is a highly skilled professional whose aim, like yours, is to produce the best possible book from the manuscript you have submitted.

The copy-editor is there to ensure that the material is correct, consistent and comprehensible in itself and to liaise with designers, production staff and typesetters to ensure that the layout and appearance of the printed book confirm and enhance those qualities. So what will the editor do to bring those qualities out to the fullest extent?

### Correctness

It is not the editor's job to vet the technical content of your manuscript or to check that you have got your facts straight. That is your job. In any case the editor will not be an expert in your subject. However, he/she will, from experience of reading and editing many books, be adept at spotting the sort of areas where technical errors may occur. He/she will query with you anything that looks suspicious – for example, statistics in one part of the book that seem to contradict statistics in another, or facts he/she is doubtful about on the basis of his/her general knowledge.

It *is* the editor's job to ensure that grammar, spelling and the use of words are correct throughout your manuscript and to check – probably by asking you – that such things as mathematical formulae are properly expressed. He/she will check, for example, that numbered headings appear in the correct sequence and that the contents pages correspond to the text itself. If he/she is doubtful about the accuracy of a quotation you have used or unsure where a particular quotation ends and your text begins again, this too will appear on the list of 'queries for the author' which will be sent to you. Typing errors will be corrected and captions to illustrations will be checked against the illustrations themselves. You will be asked to acknowledge the source of any quoted material you have not attributed.

### *Consistency*

This will claim a great deal of the copy-editor's time and attention. We have already mentioned house style: it is the copy-editor's job to ensure that it is adhered to. If you have used double quotation marks in one place and single ones in another, for example, or if you express a number once as '500' and another time as 'five hundred', these will be standardised. Similarly, if you have referred to the United Kingdom here, the British Isles there and Great Britain elsewhere, the editor will check what distinction, if any, you intend between these different terms and will amend them as necessary.

The editor will also ensure that you have observed the basic rules of structural consistency which we have already referred to in Chapter 7. If you have used only two headings in one chapter of 5,000 words and 20 in another of the same length, he/she may well suggest that a degree of harmonisation is called for. Again, if you have ranked as of equal status two headings one of which should, to conform to the internal logic of the book, be subordinate to the other, this will be amended. If you have included summaries at the end of some chapters and not others, you may be asked to provide summaries for those where they do not appear or to delete them where they do. And so on.

If you are including tables, graphs or figures, the editor will make sure that they are presented in a consistent way, with the same information shown in the same form wherever possible. If you quote figures up to 1990 in most tables and figures to 1987 in a few, or if all your graphs are bar charts except one which is a line graph, he/she will want to know if there is a genuine reason for the discrepancy. He/she will also check that the illustrations show what the text says they show and that they do not contradict one another.

### Comprehensibility

Your editor will naturally be concerned to ensure that anyone reading your book can understand what you are trying to say. If he/she is unsure what you mean in certain instances, he/she will ask you to rewrite for greater clarity. If he/she can see what you mean but feels it could be put better, he/she will reword the passage in question and will probably check with you that the meaning has not been materially altered in the process.

The editor will check that you have explained everything you need to explain and that it is not impossible to understand certain terms in Chapter 4 without having read Chapter 5. He/she may well include cross-references between different sections of the text if he/she feels they make things clearer. If you have omitted to mention something in Chapter 5 that you said in Chapter 4 you would be mentioning there, you will be asked to include it. If you have repeated passages unnecessarily in different chapters, you will be asked to delete the repetitions. If some of your illustrations serve to confuse rather than illuminate, the editor will ask for them to be improved or omitted. Alternatively, if an additional illustration might help to clarify a point you are making in the text, you may be asked to provide one.

### *Dealing with the editor's comments and queries*

It will be clear from what has been said that differences can easily arise between author and editor during this process. You will, after all, be very close to your material and will no doubt be feeling rather protective towards the words you have spent so much time and effort committing to paper over the past months.

A good editor will be sensitive to this fact. But he/she will also be approaching the manuscript with a fresh mind and a pair of eyes which, however detached you think you are able to be from your material, are likely to be more objective than your own. You should therefore take seriously any suggestions made and if, when you have considered them as dispassionately as you can, you feel that you are right and the editor is wrong, you should have strong grounds for advancing your opinion. Good editors will be as open to the views of their authors as you should be to theirs and the editorial process is inevitably to some extent a process of compromise and discussion.

There may well be times when you feel your editor is being pedantic or merely obtuse. But even at the height of your outrage it is worth pausing to remind yourself that you are both on the same side. What you both want is to produce the best possible book. And many experienced authors will admit that, however resistant they may originally have been to changes made by their editor, the resulting book was better for them in the end.

A good editor will send you a number of questions and suggestions about your manuscript when he/she has been through it. These will not represent the only changes that will have been made to it, but they will be the ones where the editor feels he/she needs your input. If your material has been extensively reworked, you may also be sent the amended manuscript. You should aim to reply to any queries and provide any new material you are asked for as promptly as you can. The sooner you can do so, the sooner your book can move on to the next stage of the production process.

### Printer's instructions

As has already been mentioned, in addition to ensuring that your manuscript is correct, consistent and comprehensible in itself, the copy-editor will also be giving the typesetters and printers instructions about how it should appear. Some of these instructions will be incorporated into the manuscript itself. This is known as 'marking up'. The editor will, for example, liaise with a designer, who may be a member of the publisher's staff or a freelance, to decide what type of lettering will be used for the text (the 'typeface'), how large it will be (the 'typesize'), how the different levels of headings will appear on the final printed page (e.g. in bold type, italic type, capitals, lower case etc.), how large the illustrations should be, and so on and so forth.

You will not normally be consulted about this part of the process, but if you have strong reasons for feeling that certain design features would be particularly appropriate or inappropriate, it would be as well to mention them to the editor at an early stage. In the final analysis, though, these will be matters for the publisher's professional and commercial judgement.

Once the manuscript has been copy-edited and designed, it is ready to be sent for typesetting. The next you will see of your book will be proofs.

## Reading your proofs

Before a book can be sent to the printers it has to be typeset, that is, retyped onto specially prepared material which will be used as the basis for the film from which the printers will print it.

A minority of publishers will have their own typesetting facilities in-house. Most, however, will use the services of external typesetters, who may or may not be associated with the printers who will eventually print the book. When the typesetting is completed, the typesetters will produce proofs of the book.

### Galleys and page proofs

Proofs are basically photocopies of the typesetting and come in either of two forms: galley proofs (also known simply as 'galleys') and page proofs. Galley proofs consist of continuous typesetting which has not yet been divided up into pages. Once they have been corrected, galley proofs have to be cut up and given page numbers and running heads (the headlines which appear at the top of every page of a printed book) to provide page proofs. For relatively straightforward books, many publishers dispense with the galley proof stage and produce page proofs straightaway (this is known as 'going straight to page').

Once they have received them from the typesetters the publishers will send you a complete set of proofs to read. (They will read a set at the same time themselves.) They may also send you a copy of the edited manuscript for you to read them against. What should you do with them?

### Corrections to proofs

The main purpose of proof-reading is to correct any typesetter's errors. It is *not* to rewrite your book. It is extraordinarily expensive to make corrections to a book at the proof stage. Even minor changes can have a very costly knock-on effect. For example, the addition of a single sentence on the first page of a 25-page chapter can result in the entire 25 pages having to be reset.

So – you should resist the temptation to make even cosmetic changes, still less to do any significant rewriting. You will probably find that this requires a considerable effort of self-control. After all, this will be the first time you have seen the book in something like the form in which it will appear before the public and it will probably be the first time you have read through all the material since you completed the manuscript some weeks earlier. There are bound to be things you wish you had said differently or not said at all. However, at this stage of the process you would be best advised to make a note of any refinements for the second edition. If you need any further encouragement to restraint, remember that you almost certainly have a clause in your contract permitting the publisher to deduct from your first royalty cheque the cost of any author's corrections above a certain percentage of the original cost of typesetting. Since the cost of corrections is proportionately much more expensive than the cost of the original setting, you can very easily cross this threshold.

If certain changes are unavoidable – for example, because developments in the world at large have rendered something you have said completely out of date or because you have spotted a genuine inaccuracy – try to make any new copy fit as precisely as possible into the same amount of space as the copy it replaces.

It is important to distinguish between typesetter's errors and any other changes when you correct your proofs. Typesetters will not charge the publishers for any typesetting errors, but they will certainly charge for any other changes they have to make. Use different coloured ink for typesetter's errors and other amendments and indicate which colour refers to which category on the first sheet of the proofs. (Red for typesetter's errors and blue for anything else is a common convention.)

There are a number of standard symbols used for proof correction and a table of these is included as Appendix 2 (see page 127). Make sure that you indicate all amendments as clearly as you can and that you mark them in the margin as well as in the text. When you return your corrected proofs to the publishers, they will collate all your amendments with their own onto one set of proofs which will then be sent to the typesetters for correction. The copy-editor will therefore need to see at a glance exactly what it is you want to change.

Apart from obvious errors such as incorrect keystrokes (e.g. 'that' for 'than'), what sort of things should you be looking out for? Common typesetter's errors include:

- transposed letters or words
- incorrect spacing between words
- repetition of sections of text

- omission of sections of text

- use of the wrong typeface or typestyle (e.g. italic instead of roman, bold instead of medium) or the wrong size of type

- incorrect indentation of lists or paragraphs

- incorrect hyphenation of words which need to be broken between the end of one line and the beginning of the next (e.g. hyp-henation instead of hyphen-ation).

If you find two or three errors in a short section of text, it is worth becoming especially vigilant. Typesetters get tired and lose concentration like other people and they tend to make mistakes in batches at these times.

When the copy-editor sends you your set of proofs he/she will usually give you a date by which he/she would like to have them back. You should make every effort to return your corrected proofs by or before that date. Publishers book their time in advance with typesetters, printers and binders and a short delay at this stage can cause a disproportionately long delay later.

If the proofs you have just read were galley proofs you may be sent page proofs once your and the publishers' corrections have been done and the galleys have been made up into pages. If the first proofs you saw were page proofs, you will probably not be sent a corrected set, although the publishers will almost certainly read one themselves.

You will normally need to work from the page proofs to prepare an index for your book. Indeed, the copy-editor may ask you to send him/her the index when you return your corrected proofs. It is therefore time to consider how you should go about drawing up an index.

## Preparing the index

The index which appears at the back of a book is a crucial part of most works of non-fiction. Only the shortest and most straight-forward books can afford to do without one. Whereas the contents list, which appears at the front, is primarily a guide to the order in which the book's contents are covered, the index is a guide to every constituent part of the book, from each occurrence of the central theme right down to the names of individuals mentioned in the text.

There are few things more irritating than trying to find your way around a long and complex book without an index. Even a very detailed contents list – and most are not very detailed – cannot make up for it. If, for example, you are reading a book on the history of the French Revolution, the contents list may tell you that there is a chapter on the Terror, but it will not help you to find every textual reference to Robespierre. The lack of a good index is very often picked up by reviewers and can damn an otherwise excellent book.

### Professional indexers

Considering that an index is so important and that there are such people as professional indexers, it is perhaps surprising that some publishers still ask their authors to prepare indexes themselves. If this is the case, you will almost certainly have a clause in your contract obliging you to submit the index within a specified time. (You may be able to ask the publishers to waive this requirement and have the index prepared professionally themselves, but they may want to deduct the cost of so doing from your royalties. If your index is prepared by a professional indexer, you should insist on seeing it before it is typeset. Indexers are experts at indexing, but may not be experts in your subject.)

### When to prepare the index

A final index cannot be prepared until you know the final page numbering of the book. If, then, you have been asked to prepare an index, you will not be able to finish it until you have seen the page proofs. (For this reason, publishers often send authors two copies of their page proofs – one for correction and the other to index from. If your publisher doesn't, it would be worth asking for two sets.) However, it is possible to make a start on the index much earlier than this if you want to. You can index from your original manuscript and make a note of the folio numbers (see page 93). Then, when the page proofs arrive, you can compare the original manuscript against them and convert the folio numbers to final page numbers as appropriate.

### How to compile the index

Whenever you decide to do your index, the basic technique is the same. Unless you have a computer system sophisticated enough to do it automatically, you will need to go through the book sentence by sentence, picking out the key words – ideas, names, places etc. – and listing them in alphabetical order. Before you start it is a good idea to look at various books on your own shelves to see how other authors have organised their indexes. In particular, it would be worth looking carefully at any books where you remember finding the index either especially helpful or especially deficient, since there will be useful lessons in both.

You may find that your editor gives you an indication of the approximate number of entries he/she would like your index to include. Since the pages of books are generally printed in groups of 32, 16 or eight (these are known as 'gatherings' or 'signatures' – if you look at the point where the pages of a book meet its spine you will usually be able to see them very clearly), publishers often know exactly how many blank pages they have left to fill after the last page of the text and will decide the length of the index accordingly. This can be a very helpful guide, but you should argue if you feel you cannot produce a worthwhile index in the space available.

Probably the best way to produce an index is the traditional one of transcribing each main entry onto a card and adding to it the number of any page on which a reference to the subject of that entry occurs. Any sub-entry can be added to the same card. For example, if your main entry is 'Robespierre', your sub-entries might read 'birth', 'first political writing', 'execution' etc. Alternatively, you might prefer to dispense with sub-entries altogether and simply list all the pages on which Robespierre is mentioned. You will have to judge which approach is most suitable, taking into account the complexity of your book, the importance of the individual entry, the likely expectations of your readers, any instructions from your publisher etc.

### What to include in the index

What determines the sort of subjects you should include in the index? This too will depend upon the book concerned. A good general rule is to test every entry for its relevance to the subject of the book and to ask yourself what you would like to be able to locate in a book of this kind if you were coming to it for the first time. For example, there would be no point having an index entry for 'Robespierre' in the book you are now reading, however many times he is mentioned in examples. No-one will pick up a book on how to get published and immediately want to know where he can find Robespierre in it!

Generally, every main heading and probably every subheading will warrant an entry of its own. As you read each paragraph under each heading, ask yourself whether there is anything specific in that paragraph which the reader might want to find, quite apart from the heading itself. If there is, make out a card for it. It can be useful to underline in the text every word or group of words for which you make out a card, especially if you are indexing from the manuscript.

### Finalising the index

When you have been through the whole book, arrange the index cards and the sub-entries under each main entry into alphabetical order. If you have been through the book in order, the page numbers you have added on each card will already be in order. If not, put them in order now. If references to any one entry cover a number of consecutive pages without a natural break, show this by noting the first and last of these pages and placing a dash between them (e.g. 13-21). When all the entries and page numbers are ordered correctly, type them out onto A4 paper, in double spacing, like the rest of the manuscript.

Your index is now complete and can be sent to the publishers for typesetting. You may or may not receive proofs of the index once it has been set. If you do, the same rules apply as for the proofs of the text itself. Do not make any amendments at this stage except to correct errors.

The index is the last part of the book to be typeset. It is also the last part of the production process with which you will be personally involved. When it is done, your work on the book is finally over and it is ready to be sent for printing and binding. Now is the time to put your feet up and wait for the finished copies.

## The book jacket

Before we go on to look briefly at the printing and binding process, it is worth saying a few words about the book jacket or, in the case of a paperback, the cover.

Publishers spend a great deal of time designing their jackets, since the appearance of a book can be a significant factor in its success or failure. Many produce jackets a long way ahead of the book itself for publicity purposes. Editors, designers and marketing staff will get together to hammer out a design; copywriters, who may be editors or publicity people, will write the 'blurb' about the book and the author which will appear on the back of the book or on the inside flaps.

It is unusual for authors to be consulted in this process, although you may well be sent a copy of the designer's initial sketch (known as a 'visual' or 'rough') or a proof of the jacket for information. You may also be asked to approve the jacket blurb, which will probably bear an uncanny resemblance to your Introduction or to the résumé you wrote for your author's questionnaire.

It is worth remembering that publishers often find it difficult to think of striking and original ideas for jacket designs and may well be grateful for your suggestions, especially if you can make them before they draw up a design themselves. In the final analysis, though, it will be their decision.

## Printing and binding

As mentioned earlier, the printing and binding are the only parts of the production process with which you will not be involved. It is nonetheless worth looking briefly at what happens once the book goes to the printer. There are a number of different printing techniques. What follows describes the most common process.

Once the typesetting is finalised it is sent to the printer in the form of 'camera-ready copy' (CRC). The CRC is first 'imposed', which means that it is organised in flat sheets, each of which corresponds to a single gathering or signature (see page 110) and which, when printed, can be folded and cut to produce pages in the order in which they will appear in the finished book. The sheets of CRC are then photographed to produce the film from which the book will be printed (hence the name camera-ready copy). This film is treated so that the areas which will appear white on the finished pages will reject the printer's ink.

When the flat sheets have been printed, they are folded and cut, so that they look like a finished book without a binding. A sample may be sent to the publisher in this form in the interests of quality control. The loose sheets are then bound into covers and, in the case of a hardback, jacketed. This is done by the binders, or increasingly, in the case of large printing firms, by the printers themselves. The finished books are then delivered to the publishers' warehouse.

The production process is now complete. You will soon hold the complimentary copies of your book, the book which began so many months ago as nothing more than an idea. You are a published author. For you, it is the end of a long and all-consuming effort. But the independent life of your book is just beginning.

# 9

# In Print

After all the intensive activity of writing your book, delivering it to the publishers, answering your editor's queries, reading your proofs and preparing an index, you may find that things suddenly become rather quiet once the book is actually published. You no longer receive phone calls, letters or packages from the publisher every few days. You no longer live in daily expectation of receiving your complimentary copies of the book. In fact, you may feel that publication is a bit of an anti-climax. You may wonder what is happening to your book now that it has suddenly become public property.

The answer is that a great deal is happening. In particular, the publishers' marketing campaign will be moving into top gear.

A short period may elapse between the delivery of your book to the publishers' warehouse and its technical publication date. If the book forms a particularly important part of their publishing programme, the publishers may stage some kind of publication event, such as a launch party or a press reception, at which you may be asked to say a few words. It is more likely, though, that the book will simply start to appear in bookshops and libraries and friends will start to phone you up to say they have seen it. So what exactly are the publishers doing to sell your book and how will it affect you?

# The marketing campaign

As was said in Chapter 1, the two basic techniques of marketing that are used to sell books are direct selling and selling through the book trade. In addition to these, the publishers will be sending out review copies of your book, trying to get media coverage where appropriate and seeking to sell subsidiary rights if they feel there is scope for so doing. All these matters are normally the responsibility of the marketing department and we shall look at each of them briefly in a moment.

First, though, a general point: the extent to which publishers involve their authors in the marketing of their books varies according to the publisher and the type of book. Some may set up a meeting with you shortly before publication to discuss the marketing of your book in a little more detail. Your author's questionnaire will probably serve as a basis for this meeting. This is an excellent opportunity for you to put forward any ideas you may have for special marketing approaches and for the publishers to clarify any points they are unsure about. For example, if they are intending to launch a direct mail campaign for your book, they may wish to seek your advice about the precise job titles of the people to whom they will be sending information about it. They may also find it useful to have the names of people who may be interested in reviewing the book, in addition to their own lists of contacts in the press and other media.

There may also be other opportunities to become involved in publicising your book – for example, if you are speaking at conferences on the subject. Do not be shy about pointing out these sorts of possibility to the publishers. At the same time, do not try to tell them how to do their job. Most publishers have highly professional marketing and sales staff who know their field extremely well. Ask yourself in what respects your book might be different from those the publisher has already produced and make sure any suggestions you make relate to these characteristics.

### Direct sales

Direct sales are sales made direct to the customer as a result of mail shots or advertising or such techniques as telephone selling. For books which have an easily identifiable and accessible specialist market, direct marketing can be a very effective, if expensive, way of making sales. The typical direct mail shot would consist of a leaflet about the book, or about a group of books, together with a covering letter.

Publishers may also place advertisements or loose inserts in relevant journals or newspapers. This too is an expensive way of reaching potential buyers but can be very effective for books aimed at professional markets.

### Trade sales

Trade sales are sales made to bookshops or other retailers. They may also include sales made to library suppliers, who sell on to libraries, or to libraries themselves. They constitute the main body of sales for all but the most specialist kinds of publication.

Most publishers will have their own force of sales reps who sell books to these kinds of outlet. Again, these are generally highly professional people. There is no need to telephone the publisher at regular intervals to point out that your book is not stocked at your local bookshop or at an airport bookstall. Many specialist works of non-fiction never find their way into general bookshops because the booksellers would never have any call for them.

### Reviews

Immediately upon publication, the publisher's marketing people will send review copies of your book to all the newspapers and journals which may be interested in it. Most publishers will have strong links with the editors of such publications, but this does not by any means guarantee that every book they send will get reviewed. Editors – especially those on the national papers – are deluged with books and can only review a small number of them. There is no point in the publisher trying to pressurise them. Quite rightly, they will value their editorial independence and will resist any such approach. It may take some months for reviews of your book to appear.

Review copies may also be sent to the editors of relevant television programmes or local radio stations. If you are lucky and your book captures their imagination, you may find yourself being asked to give an interview. If this happens at all, it is likely to be immediately after publication while the book is still current news.

If your book is relevant to particular academic courses, the publishers may also send out 'inspection copies' to the teachers of those courses. These are designed to enable the teachers to decide whether or not to 'adopt' the book as a recommended text. Adoptions of this kind are crucial to the success of academic publishers.

Before leaving the subject of review copies, a final word of warning: you will have been sent six or so complimentary copies of your book on publication. Be careful not to give them all away. Many people will have helped you write your book, if only by keeping out of your way and putting up with your bad moods on the days when you thought it would never get finished. You can probably think of more than six people you would like to have a copy of the final work. It is only too easy to end up with no copies for yourself. Remember: after your six free copies have gone you will have to pay for any others. You may be able to persuade the publishers to send review copies to people who you feel could generate useful publicity, but they will be wary of doing so unless they see a likelihood of tangible returns. They will certainly not be happy about sending free copies to your boss or your bank manager. If you feel they should have a copy, you will have to send one from your own supply.

## Subsidiary rights

If there is scope for an overseas edition of your book, or if it has potential for serialisation or for sale to a book club, the publishers' marketing staff will now be trying to sell these rights. With the average work of non-fiction, the scope for doing so is generally very limited. You will see very few people walking around in *How to Get Published* tee-shirts!

## Royalty payments

Your royalties will be paid at regular intervals – generally either six-monthly or yearly – as specified in your contract. You will normally receive your first cheque within a few weeks of the end of the first accounting period after your book is published, assuming the accrued royalties exceed the amount of your advance and any other sums the publisher may be deducting from your royalty account (such as the cost of typesetting your corrections to the proofs – see page 67).

The statement which accompanies this cheque will show you the number of sales that have been made to date. It may separate these into sales made in the home market and sales made overseas and it may also indicate the number of books which have been returned unsold by bookshops (who buy stock on a sale or return basis). Remember that the publishers will have made a lot of the sales at a discount on the cover price. Your total royalty will therefore not necessarily be equal to the total number of books sold multiplied by the published price of the book.

Remember too that royalty income is not taxed at source. You will therefore have to declare your royalty earnings on your next tax return. Be sure to keep a note of the amounts and the dates of payment.

## Public Lending Right

Every year more than 600 million loans of books are made from public libraries in the United Kingdom. The Public Lending Right (PLR) scheme is designed to give authors some income from the use of their book by people who borrow it from public libraries. If you are resident in the U.K. or the Federal Republic of Germany you may be eligible to register your book under the PLR scheme.

The scheme works by selecting a sample of public libraries (currently 20) which is changed every few years. The libraries record the number of times a given book is borrowed in a year and this number is used as a basis for extrapolating an estimated figure for borrowings of the book throughout the country. The author of the book is then paid a small sum per borrowing, these payments being made once a year. Each new edition of a book counts as a separate publication for the purposes of the calculation, and registration lasts for 50 years after the author's death even if the author is not the copyright holder. Co-authors, illustrators, translators and editors of works compiled from contributions may also be eligible to register.

Although the sum per book is small, it is surprising how quickly it can mount up. It would be well worth writing to the Registrar of the PLR for further details and to establish whether or not you are eligible. The address is The PLR Office, Bayheath House, Prince Regent Street, Stockton-on-Tees, Cleveland TS18 1DF.

## The Society of Authors

The Society of Authors is one of two trade unions for authors in the U.K., the other being the Writers' Guild of Great Britain (see page 120 below). It exists to advise and represent its members and to protect their rights, particularly in respect of their dealings with publishers and the Government.

There are two categories of membership of the Society – full and associate. Full membership is open to authors who have had a full-length work published in the U.K., associate membership to those who have had a full-length work accepted for publication but not yet published and to those who have had some types of shorter work published.

The Society is able to provide information about the whole publishing and book business, and produces a number of useful short guides to such matters as copyright and VAT. It will also advise on negotiations with publishers and provides a contract vetting service.  Under some circumstances it will even take legal action on behalf of individual members.

Further information about the Society is available from the Membership Secretary, The Society of Authors, 84 Drayton Gardens, London SW10 9SB .

## The Writers' Guild of Great Britain

The Writers' Guild of Great Britain grew out of the Screenwriters' Guild, but now represents all types of freelance writer.  Unlike the Society of Authors, it is affiliated to the TUC, but like the Society it pays no political levy.  It too exists to represent and advise its members.

Membership is open to anyone who has had a full-length work published and also to anyone who has received a contract for publication of a full-length work.  The Guild is therefore able to advise on contractual terms for first-time authors who apply for membership.

Further information about the Guild is available from the Membership Secretary, The Writers' Guild of Great Britain, 430 Edgware Road, London W2 1EH .

## Writing new editions

As mentioned earlier, most publishers' contracts cover not just the first edition of a book but all future editions as well.  When your book is published,  both you and the publishers will be hoping that it will be successful enough to remain in print for many years and run to many editions.  How do such editions come about and what will they mean for you?

### Publishers' backlists

Publishers keep a watchful eye on their stock figures in order to be able to predict when they are likely to run out of copies of a particular book. (Publishers refer to books already published as their 'backlist', and backlist management is an important part of any commissioning editor's job.) When continuing demand for a book indicates that more copies of it will be needed than were originally printed, there are basically two courses of action publishers can take. They can reprint the book with no or very few amendments, or they can produce a new, fully revised edition.

Which of these routes the publishers take will depend mainly on how much has changed in the world since the book was originally published. In some areas, such as the law, the sciences or politics, events can move very rapidly and a book may be out of date within a year or so of publication. In these areas, publishers will normally set their print-runs with the likely pace of change firmly in mind. In other fields a book can have a shelf life of many years without becoming obsolete. Since most commissioning editors are not experts in the fields in which they commission, they will generally want to consult their authors about the likely level of change needed to keep a book up to date. If, then, your book looks as if it will be out of stock in, say, a year's time, and the demand for it makes it worth printing more copies, you will probably be asked by your commissioning editor whether the text needs to be revised and, if so, to what extent.

### Revising the text

If changes are necessary, you will normally come to an agreement with the publisher about the date by which you will deliver the revised copy. It is unusual for publishers to renegotiate a contract for a new edition, but you may find they are prepared to offer an additional advance against royalties, especially if you will incur significant research or secretarial costs in compiling it. As was mentioned in Chapter 5, your contract may also include an escalator clause, giving you a higher royalty rate after the first edition of the book has been sold. While it may appear to you that you are effectively writing a new edition free of charge, then, you should remember that you will in fact be getting the same or higher level of payment on it for what will almost certainly be much less work than was involved in writing the original book.

The golden rule where new editions are concerned is to *start keeping a file of changes as soon as your book is published*. In the immediate glow of satisfaction that follows the arrival of your complimentary copies, it is easy to forget that while this may be the end of one era in your life as an author, it may also be the start of another. Set aside a file straightaway for any newspaper or magazine cuttings relating to the subject of the book which you may come across. Make a note of any suggestions made by friends or colleagues or by readers who have written to you. Note too any mistakes you may have noticed in the printed book – there can be few books printed in which there are no mistakes at all – and any refinements which you wish you could have made at the proof stage or which have occurred to you since. It will be very much easier, when you get a call from your editor in, say, two years' time, to go through the file and assess the likely level of changes, than to have to try to recall everything relevant that has happened since the book was published.

The publishers will probably send you a photocopy of the pages of the book on A4 paper. This will enable you to make any amendments in the margins of the text. You should type all your amendments and key them into the text as clearly as possible. If any changes run to more than a sentence or two, type them on a separate sheet of paper and place it after the page on which the amendment will appear. Head the new sheet '– A', where – is the number of the page on which the amendment will appear, and write against the precise point on that page where you want the amendment to be incorporated into the text 'Take in copy from p – A'.

For amendments longer than a paragraph or two, especially if there are a number of them in a short space, retype the whole section in which they will appear and delete from the photocopy the section your new typescript replaces. Head the replacement sheets ' – A', ' – B' etc., where – is the number of the first page of the deleted section, and insert the sheets after that page. Write against the deletion copy 'Take in copy from pp – A, – B [etc.]'.

The production process for the new edition will be similar to that for the original book (see Chapter 8), although it is unlikely that your revised manuscript will be put out to an external reader. You should certainly expect to see proofs of the new edition and to produce a revised index.

## Your next book...?

You have written your book and had it published. You have seen an idea grow from its speculative beginnings into a solid printed work, from a private ambition into a public property. You have had the satisfaction of knowing that people have bought and read your words, perhaps even in sufficient numbers to have warranted new editions. You can add 'author' to your other qualifications. What now?

The experience of publishing may have left you determined never to write another book for as long as you live. Alternatively, it may have whetted your appetite for authorship and publication. You may look towards full-time authorship as a future way of life. If so, remember that there are very few professional authors. The authorial life is an insecure and often lonely one. In relation to the time put in, the financial returns can be small and a long time coming. And are there enough things you can write about to make it a practicable option?

But your experience of getting published will have shown you that there is no need to be a full-time author in order to write and publish books. For many people there are few working satisfactions comparable to that of seeing themselves in print. And once you are published, you may well find yourself in a stronger position to interest your existing publisher or others in your next project. There are no corners you can cut: you will have to go through all the same processes you went through to get your first book published. But you do now have a track record as an author.

Is there another book in you...?

# Appendix 1: Glossary of publishing terms

**acquisitions editor**   see *commissioning editor*

**adoptions**   books recommended for use on particular college courses

**advance**   payment made to an author on account against *royalty* payments

**artwork**   finished material, either for text or artwork, from which the film for printing the book will be made up (see also *camera-ready copy*)

**backlist**   a publisher's existing published books

**blurb**   description of the book on its back cover or inside jacket flap

**blues**   see ozalids

**bold**   heavy type; indicated by wavy underlining in *manuscript*

**camera-ready copy**   finished typesetting, on special material, from which the film for printing the book will be made up (also known as CRC)

**cased**   hardback (see also *cloth*)

**cloth**   hardback (see also *cased*)

**commissioning editor**   member of the publishing team responsible for initiating and developing books (also known variously as *acquisitions editor*, *sponsoring editor* or simply *editor*); the *commissioning editor* is generally responsible for a particular subject area of the publisher's *list*

**copy**   textual material, particularly in *manuscript* form

**copy-editor**   member of the publishing team responsible for preparing *manuscripts* for the printer (also known variously as *desk editor*, *house editor*, *sub-editor* or simply *editor*)

**copyright**   system of legal protection for an author's published or unpublished material

**cover price**   price at which a published book is sold to members of the public

**CRC**   see *camera-ready copy*

**desk editor**   see *copy-editor*

**editor**   either a *commissioning editor* or a *copy-editor*

**em**   measurement of unit of type, equivalent to the horizontal space occupied by a single letter m

**escalator clause**   clause in a publishing contract by which the author receives an increased *royalty* after a certain number of copies of a book have been sold

**extent**   length of a book

**folio**   sheet of *manuscript;* also page number of book

**font**   set of type with the same *typesize* and *typeface*

**format**   size and shape of a printed book

**galley proofs**   *proofs* in the form of continuous *typesetting*, undivided into pages (also known simply as *galleys*); see also *page proofs*

**galleys**   see *galley proofs*

**gathering**   group of pages printed together (also known as *signature*)

**grids** sheets of card, corresponding to the size of the printed page, onto which *camera-ready copy* is pasted to provide *page proofs*

**half-title** page in the *prelims* bearing the title of the work only; normally two pages before the *title page*

**half-tones** black-and-white photographs as illustrations in a printed book

**house editor** see *copy-editor*

**house style** stylistic and presentational rules observed by a publishing house in all its publications; see also *style sheet*

**inspection copies** books sent out free of charge by the publisher, normally to academics and other teachers, with a view to achieving *adoptions* on particular courses

**italic** sloping type; indicated by single underlining of words in *manuscript*

**limp** paperback

**list** publisher's published *titles,* either generally or in a particular subject area (e.g. business list, sports list)

**literary agent** professional acting on behalf of an author in his/her dealings with publishers

**looseleaf** type of publication in which pages are not conventionally bound but are issued with a ring-binder; buyers normally subscribe to an updating service

**manuscript** typescript or word-processed material, usually as delivered by an author; never handwritten material

**marking up** marking the *manuscript* with design instructions for the typesetter or printer

**medium** normal density type (compare *bold*)

**MS** normal abbreviation for *manuscript*

**ozalids** film proofs (also known as *blues*)

**page, going straight to** producing *page proofs* without producing *galley proofs* first

**page proofs** proofs in the form of *typesetting* already divided up into pages (compare *galley proofs*)

**paste-up** the process of producing final *artwork* by pasting *camera-ready copy* onto *grids*

**perfect binding** form of paperback binding in which pages are glued rather than sewn to a book's spine (compare *sewn binding*)

**point** unit of measurement for size of type

**prelims** pages preliminary to the main text in a printed book

**print-run** the number of copies of a book printed in any one printing

**proofs** photocopies of the *typesetting* for a book; see also *galley proofs* and *page proofs*

**readers** people retained by the publisher to review *manuscripts* and proposals with a view to advising on their quality and saleability

**recto** each right-hand page of a printed book (compare *verso*)

**roman**    plain upright type (compare *italic*)

**royalty**    percentage of the publisher's receipts from sales of a book paid to its author

**running heads**    headlines which normally appear at the top of every page of a printed book (often giving the title of the book or the title of the chapter)

**setting**    see *typesetting*

**sewn binding**    form of binding in which the pages are sewn to a book's spine (compare *perfect binding*)

**signature**    see *gathering*

**specification**    the detailed design brief for a book (indicating type and size of paper, type and size of type, type of binding, etc.)

**sponsoring editor**    see *commissioning editor*

**style sheet**    document embodying the publisher's *house style*

**sub-editor**    see *copy-editor*

**subsidiary rights**    rights to use of published material sold by the publisher to third parties (e.g. translation rights, broadcasting rights, serialisation rights, book-club rights, etc.)

**title**    published or commissioned book

**title page**    page in the *prelims* usually bearing the full title of the work and the name of its author and publisher; see also *half-title*

**trade**    the book trade; also used to describe the sort of books which are sold almost exclusively through bookshops

**typeface**    a specific design of type

**typesetting**    the process and physical result of retyping the book into a form in which it can be used for printing; also known simply as *setting*

**typesize**    the size of a *typeface*

**typestyle**    the style of individual words in a *typeface* (e.g. *bold*, *medium*, *italic*)

**vanity publishers**    publishers who publish books in return for payments from authors

**verso**    each left-hand page of a printed book (compare *recto*)

## Proof-reading signs

| Instruction | Textual Mark | Marginal Mark |
|---|---|---|
| Correction is concluded | None | / |
| Leave unchanged | – – – – – under character to remain | Ⓙ |
| Insert in text the matter indicated in the margin | ⋏ | New matter followed by ⋏ |
| Insert additional matter identified by a letter in a diamond | ⋏ | ⋏ Followed by ◇Ⓐ for example |
| Delete | / through character(s) or ⊢——⊣ through word(s) to be deleted | ♂ |
| Delete and close up | ⌢ through character or ⊂⊃ through character e.g. chara͡cter | ♂ |
| Substitute character or substitute part of one or more word(s) | / through character or ⊢————⊣ through word(s) | New character or new word(s) |
| Wrong fount. Replace by character(s) of correct fount | Encircle character(s) to be changed | ⊗ |
| Change damaged character(s) | Encircle character(s) to be changed | ✕ |
| Set in or change to italic | ——— under character(s) to be set or changed | ⊔ |
| Set in or change to capital letters | ≡≡≡ under character(s) to be set or changed | ≡ |
| Set in or change to small capital letters | ≡≡≡ under character(s) to be set or changed | ═ |
| Set in or change to bold type | ∿∿∿ under character(s) to be set or changed | ∿ |
| Change capital letters to lower case letters | Encircle character(s) to be changed | ≢ |
| Change italic to upright type | Encircle character(s) to be changed | ⊔ |
| Invert type | Encircle character to be inverted | ↻ |
| Substitute or insert full stop or decimal point | / through character or ⋏ where required | ⊙ |
| Substitute or insert semi-colon | / through character or ⋏ where required | ; |
| Substitute or insert comma | / through character or ⋏ where required | , |

| Instruction | Textual Mark | Marginal Mark |
|---|---|---|
| Start new paragraph | | |
| Run on (no new paragraph) | | |
| Centre | [enclosing matter to be centred] | [ ] |
| Indent | | |
| Cancel indent | | |
| Move matter specified distance to the right | enclosing matter to be moved to the right | |
| Take over character(s), word(s) or line to next line, column or page | | |
| Take back character(s), word(s) or line to previous line, column or page | | |
| Correct horizontal alignment | Single line above and below misaligned matter e.g.<br><br>mi sal ig ned | |
| Close up. Delete space between characters or words | linking characters | |
| Insert space between characters | \| between characters affected | |
| Insert space between words | between words affected | |
| Reduce space between characters | \| between characters affected | |
| Reduce space between words | between words affected | |
| Make space appear equal between characters or words | \| between characters or words affected | |